Faith Talk
Journaling With God

A Journey of Christian Faith

Volume I

Authored by Christian Life Coaching by LtA

Published by KHARIS PUBLISHING, imprint of KHARIS MEDIA LLC.

Copyright © 2019 Christian Life Coaching by LtA

ISBN-13: 978-1-946277-25-1
ISBN-10:1- 1-946277-25-8

All rights reserved. This book or parts thereof may not be reproduced in any form, stored in a retrieval system, or transmitted in any form by any means - electronic, mechanical, photocopy, recording, or otherwise - without prior written permission of the publisher, except as provided by United States of America copyright law.

Scripture quotations marked (NIV) are taken from the Holy Bible, New International Version®, NIV®. Copyright © 1973, 1978, 1984, 2011 by Biblica, Inc.™ Used by permission of Zondervan. All rights reserved worldwide. www.zondervan.com The "NIV" and "New International Version" are trademarks registered in the United States Patent and Trademark Office by Biblica, Inc.™

All KHARIS PUBLISHING products are available at special quantity discounts for bulk purchase for sales promotions, premiums, fund-raising, and educational needs. For details, write:

Kharis Media LLC
Tel: 1-479-599-8657
support@kharispublishing.com
www.kharispublishing.com

ENDORSEMENTS FOR *FAITH TALK*

"I have asked LtA to pen a Bible study for years! If you are interested in being equipped to go out and make disciples and have a truly impactful witness, LtA's teaching style is perfect for you. I have learned a great deal from this spirit filled Christian Life Coach and am excited for anyone who will pick up this new teaching series on journaling with God and dive into the Word." Char M., Detroit, MI.

"Having a Christian Life Coach walk you through life's struggles has been such a gift to me and everyone around me. LtA helps guide you in order for the Holy Spirit to bring revelation into your heart. I have never had so much fun reading the Bible before! You will only benefit from spending time in the Word, and with a guided tour by LtA, that time will be well spent." Laura R., Columbia, MO.

"The teachings of Christian Life Coaching by LtA are very inspirational to me. I find the combination of thoughts, scripture, and graphics used in each social media post easy to meditate upon and restful to my soul. The regular Bible trivia questions are also a great deal of fun! Ongoing Bible study is important to me and I am pleased that a Bible study program is being put together in this similar style of teaching." Leslie M., Arlington, VA.

"I am looking forward to reading more from Christian Life Coaching by LtA. When I was experiencing a very difficult time in my life I read LtA's helpful guide about listening to the Holy Spirit during quiet times. I found encouragement, spirit-filled and thought-provoking guidance. I am happy to say that I have revisited my spiritual gifts and it helped me find my way. I'm very grateful and trust that the information provided to me will help others as well." J. Love, St. Louis, MO.

"If walking out your salvation has been challenging for you, then LtA will unlock the keys to this mystery. LtA has a straightforward teaching style and no stone will be left unturned. I have learned a great deal from this divinely sent Christian Life Coach and cannot wait to begin journaling with God!" L.K., Colorado Springs, CO
I find the writings of Christian Life Coaching by LtA very well thought out

and inspirational. Christian Life Coaching by LtA provides more than just teachings, they go in depth into the meanings behind the scriptures and how it relates to our lives today." C. Ashby, Annandale, VA.

"If you have had a slump in your Christian walk and need a buoy of faith, LtA is a great teacher. LtA helps you implement practical solutions to your everyday walk with Jesus. LtA provides tools to go deeper in Christ and feel a renewed connection to your Savior. After working with LtA, my journey with Christ is back on track and my intimacy with God is much stronger. I am excited to start journaling with God!" S. Rob, Denver, CO.

"If you have ever wondered how God could use you, LtA will help you find that calling. LtA has been a great mentor for me. LtA gives your practical advice based on God's promises in the Bible. I have never felt closer to the Lord. I am pleased to recommend LtA's new Bible study devotional/interactive journal to anyone desiring more intimacy with the Lord." K.L., San Diego, CA

CONTENTS

1. Preface — 3
2. Introduction — 4
3. Faith, Hope and Love — 6
4. Forgiveness and Grace — 156
5. Trials and Joy — 251
6. Conclusion — 350

DEDICATION

Faith Talk: Journaling with God, a Journey of Christian Faith series is dedicated to anyone struggling under the sway of the world. I have heard too many times from friends and family, "why can't you just get along?" The answer is simple: I was pursued by God, set aside, called to a higher purpose. I will act, sound and look different from everyone else because I love God and my reputation with Him is more important to me than winning people's approval.

Believers have a lot to offer in His name. We can be transformed by the power of God AND enjoy our journey with Christ. See yourself the way God sees you, not the way the enemy describes you. Our fight is not against the world and the people in it but with the principalities and powers described in the Bible. We need to learn how to fight these spiritual battles from a position of victory through the blood of Christ and His Word. The struggle is real, and when you choose to lay your foundation on the Word of God, you too will be able to withstand what the enemy throws at you and come out on the other side intact and stronger than ever!

RISE above your ashes and be who Christ has called you to be! May you grow in your understanding so that you walk in His Love, His Truth, His Power, His Mercy, His Righteousness and His Redeeming Grace.
Whether you are just beginning your journey of Christian faith or you have been walking with the Lord for years, I pray that your journey with Christ continues to be enriched in intimacy and Truth as you walk and talk together.

PREFACE

May His grace and peace be with every reader. This book was inspired by the Holy Spirit and is dedicated to every Christian that desires deeper intimate fellowship with the Lord.

Yes beloved, everyone deserves a deep, powerful and life changing relationship with God.

We can't defeat what we don't understand. The enemy of our soul wants us to sacrifice the victory of our Christian life through his deception. Our battle is with an angel who has a God complex; not with God or people. God gave us spiritual armor to face the enemy victoriously. When we no longer lack endurance, knowledge, or clarity we can fight back and not allow our enemy to get a foothold. When we are no longer ignorant of the enemy's schemes, we grow in Christlikeness. My goal is to help uncomplicate what the enemy complicates. Because of my personal desire to understand the value of what Jesus died to give me, my ministry was developed to help people make lasting breakthroughs, win spiritual battles, unlock prison doors, build their spiritual pantry, and help them finish their race.

I will be praying for all readers of this book. My desire is that *Faith Talk: Journaling with God. A Journey of Christian Faith Volume I* will be a lifeline to readers who may feel out of sync with Jesus; and I also pray this book will be a source of encouragement. I pray you connect with Jesus, God's Word and your Bible in a powerful way!

Jeremiah 1:5 *"Before I formed you in the womb I knew you, before you were born I set you apart; I appointed you as a prophet to the nations."*

INTRODUCTION

"All Scripture is God-breathed and is useful for teaching, rebuking, correcting and training in righteousness, [17] so that the servant of God may be thoroughly equipped for every good work." **2 Timothy 3:16-17**.

It is by the Scriptures the Holy Spirit teaches us how to love and live a life of obedience by faith in response to His grace. It is therefore essential for you to be thoroughly equipped and prepared for every good work.

Faith Talk: Journaling with God. A Journey of Christian Faith Volume I is designed to help you use the Scriptures more effectively in your everyday life. The chapters are arranged so the significance of each passage is easily relatable to the topic being discussed. My prayer is that this book will help you use Scripture more effectively and gain wisdom, comfort, joy, peace and overall well-being for God's glory.

Transformation is not a one-time event; it occurs daily as you walk out your salvation. God is interested in everything you have going on in your life - what's on your mind, your pain, your joy, your struggles and your victories. You no longer have to believe that your life is dictated by your circumstances nor be swayed by worldly influences. God is the holder of all wisdom and He wants to share this wisdom supernaturally with you. Will you invite Him into your life in a more personal way and begin a new way of thinking and acting?

As you read the devotionals, meditate on the suggested scriptures and begin journaling through the discussion questions, you will enjoy a new, deeper, intimate fellowship with God which will buoy your faith and enrich your daily walk with Him.

Have your Bible open as you begin each journaling session and meditate on what the Holy Spirit reveals to you. This will most likely require you to have a quiet place and set aside time to allow the Word of God to penetrate you.

I pray your intimacy with God and your relationship with Him will strengthen and deepen as you spend this time with Him and meditate on

His Word. Time with the Lord is never wasted; include the Lord in your transformational process!

Once you experience Him fully, you can affect the people around you with a powerful testimony and help raise up disciples. *Journaling with God* in the form of a devotional/ interactive journal will be a transformation of a lifetime!

Psalm 139:16 *"Your eyes saw my unformed body; all the days ordained for me were written in your book before one of them came to be."*

Let's begin…

Faith, Hope and Love.

FAITH TALK

Why is it important to have faith, hope and love in our Christian walk? Faith, hope and love are united. Paul tells us in 1 Corinthians 13:13 that these three spiritual gifts remain *"And now these three remain: faith, hope and love. But the greatest of these is love."* In other words, some spiritual gifts will fade away but these three are permanent and need to be desired and cultivated. These gifts will be ours throughout eternity.

Praying this section will show God's goodness to all who believe and have been given the privilege of these lasting gifts.

Christian Life Coaching by LtA

Image: Thoom/Shutterstock.com

Thank and Praise

My complaining stops now! My thoughts and words
will express thanksgiving.

My heart is full of gratitude.
What power do your thoughts and words hold in the spirit world?

_____
_____
_____
_____
_____
_____
_____
_____

Yielding to the flesh will produce all kinds of results, but when the Holy Spirit controls our lives, He produces the kind of fruit that is pleasing to God.
What fruit of the Spirit does complaining exhibit? What fruit of the spirit does thanksgiving exhibit?

_____
_____
_____
_____
_____
_____
_____
_____

"They were also to stand every morning to **thank and praise** *the LORD. They were to do the same in the evening"*

1 Chronicles 23:30

Unfailing Love

The love of God brings me great peace and I am
very grateful for His promises.

Do you keep your promises? What happens to your reputation as a Christian when you don't follow through with your promises?

_____
_____
_____
_____
_____
_____
_____
_____

Would you experience a crisis of faith if God didn't keep His promises?

_____
_____
_____
_____
_____
_____
_____

"Though the mountains be shaken and the hills be removed, yet my **unfailing love** *for you will not be shaken nor my covenant of peace be removed,' says the* LORD, *who has compassion on you."*

Isaiah 54:10

FAITH TALK

Steadfast Spirit

God does not expect me to change myself
in my own strength. His refining ongoing
work in my life will be worth it!

How do you feel when you attempt to change yourself? Are you successful?

_____
_____
_____
_____
_____
_____
_____
_____

The world tells us we need to buy self-help books to change our lives. Why does self-help frequently fail?

_____
_____
_____
_____
_____
_____
_____
_____

"Create in me a pure heart, O God, and renew a **steadfast spirit** *within me."*

Psalm 51:10

Jubilee - Paid in full
Those I feel owe me shall be pardoned!

How does forgiving also free you from the debt?

_____
_____
_____
_____
_____
_____
_____
_____

Is there anyone you need to ask forgiveness from?

_____
_____
_____
_____
_____
_____
_____
_____

"Consecrate the fiftieth year and proclaim liberty throughout the land to all its inhabitants.
It shall be a **jubilee for you;** *each of you is to return to your family property and to your own clan."*

Leviticus 25:10

FAITH TALK

Freely Give
Because God freely loves me
I will freely love others.

How is love a verb?

_____
_____
_____
_____
_____
_____
_____
_____

In Luke 10 God commands us to love. The love God wants us to express is not an emotional feeling; it is a volitional love based on a decision to love.
List a few ways you can grow in your love for God and for people:

_____
_____
_____
_____
_____
_____
_____
_____

"Heal the sick, raise the dead, cleanse those who have leprosy, drive out demons. Freely you have received;
freely give."

Matthew 10:8

Be Still

Satan may roam about, but my Defender is
the Lion of Judah Who fights for me!

Do you believe you have an enemy? Do you believe you have a Defender? If so, describe each:

_____
_____
_____
_____
_____
_____

Do you believe it is the Lord's battle? Are you wearing yourself out trying to fight battles that are already won?

_____
_____
_____
_____
_____
_____

"The LORD *will fight for you; you need only to* **be still**."

Exodus 4:14

FAITH TALK

Eyes of Your Heart

I am able to fulfill the calling
the Lord has placed on me
because of my inheritance in Christ.

When does your eternal living begin?

_____
_____
_____
_____
_____
_____
_____

Is your inheritance available to you now or only in heaven?

_____
_____
_____
_____
_____
_____
_____
_____

"I pray that the **eyes of your heart** *may be enlightened in order that you may know the hope to which he has called you, the riches of his glorious inheritance in his holy people"*

Ephesians 1:8

Christian Life Coaching by LtA

Altogether Beautiful

Youth is fleeting and our bodies change,
our true beauty flows from
our heart and is refined with age.

Describe the nature of change.

_____
_____
_____
_____
_____
_____
_____
_____

List how your beauty is changing:

_____
_____
_____
_____
_____
_____
_____
_____

"You are **altogether beautiful,** *my darling;
there is no flaw in you."*

Song of Solomon 4:7

FAITH TALK

Miracles of Long Ago

God continues to perform miracles and
no challenge I face
will cause me to fear.

Do you demonstrate your faith even when you haven't been delivered from your difficult circumstance?

_____
_____
_____
_____
_____
_____
_____
_____
_____
_____

What challenges are you currently undertaking?

_____
_____
_____
_____
_____
_____
_____
_____
_____
_____

"I will remember the deeds of the LORD; *yes, I will remember your* **miracles of long ago.**"

Psalm 77:11

Perfect Peace

When I put my cares in His hands,
my soul finds comfort.

Are the people in your life able to see your hope that the best is yet to come?

_____
_____
_____
_____
_____
_____
_____

Do presently have any worldly cares? List any cares you need to cast?

_____
_____
_____
_____
_____
_____
_____

"You will keep in **perfect peace** those whose **minds** are steadfast, because they trust in you."

Isaiah 26:3

FAITH TALK

Lack No Good Thing

Thank You God for all I have-
I trust You for what I need.

Trust is built over time. When we choose to trust, we are willing to become vulnerable and enter into a deeper communication.

What did your faith in God look like when you first believed?

_____
_____
_____
_____
_____
_____
_____
_____
_____
_____

List as many blessings you can think of:

_____
_____
_____
_____
_____
_____
_____
_____

*"The lions may grow weak and hungry,
but those who seek the Lord*
lack no good thing."

Psalm 34:10

The Earth Will Give Birth

I can face whatever today brings
because He lives – in His hands I confidently rest.

Do you believe God modeled rest, and that we can rest in Him?

_____
_____
_____
_____
_____
_____
_____

What can you place in God's hands today so you can rest?

_____
_____
_____
_____
_____
_____
_____

"But your dead will live, Lord; their bodies will rise—
let those who dwell in the dust
wake up and shout for joy—
your dew is like the dew of the morning;
the earth will give birth to her dead."

Isaiah 26:19

FAITH TALK

His Coming

Today is preparation for anything
that might come my way.

What can you do today that will better prepare you for the future?

_____
_____
_____
_____
_____
_____
_____
_____

Finish this sentence: The more clearly I see the brokenness, in and around me, I will:

_____
_____
_____
_____
_____
_____
_____
_____

"Therefore, with minds that are alert and fully sober, set your hope on the grace to be brought to you when Jesus Christ is revealed at **his coming.**"

1 Peter 1:13

Abundance

Peace and hope filled me
when the love of God saved me.

Are there obstacles to pursuing peace? If so, is that a commentary on your faith?
___
___
___
___
___
___
___
___

What peace and hope are you feeling right now?
___
___
___
___
___
___
___
___

"Mercy, peace and love be yours in **abundance**."

Jude 1:2

FAITH TALK

Treasures In Heaven

The legacy I leave is not what's
engraved in a headstone;
it's Who I've knitted into others' lives.

Who have you shared the Gospel with recently?

_____
_____
_____
_____
_____
_____
_____
_____

In Mark 16 the power to witness is a result of the work of Holy Spirit. If you are telling your testimony, no one can argue with you because it is yours to tell.
Explain how you are a sharing the gospel message as the product of these Truths:

_____
_____
_____
_____
_____
_____
_____

[20] "*But store up for yourselves* **treasures in heaven**, *where moths and vermin do not destroy, and where thieves do not break in and steal.*
[21] *For where your treasure is, there your heart will be also.*"

Matthew 6:20-21

Christian Life Coaching by LtA

Stoops Down

His love bent down so I could be
raised and filled with His grace.

What does it mean to you that Jesus died for you?

_____
_____
_____
_____
_____
_____
_____
_____

When did you come to terms that the Bible points the way to victory through salvation by faith in Christ?

_____
_____
_____
_____
_____
_____
_____
_____

> [5] *"Who is like the Lord our God, the One who sits enthroned on high,*
>
> [6] *who* **stoops down** *to look on the heavens and the earth?"*
>
> Psalm 113:5-6

FAITH TALK

In Us

I will not let love only flow to me.
I will be a funnel and
let love flow through me.

What opportunities do you have to let God's love flow through you?

_____
_____
_____
_____
_____
_____
_____
_____

Have you ever knowingly let an opportunity pass without answering the call? Why?

_____
_____
_____
_____
_____
_____
_____
_____

*"No one has ever seen God; but if we love one another, God lives in us and his love is made complete **in us**."*

1 John 4:12

Tears

My tears are not lost
God collects them.

How does knowing that God collects your tears affect your shedding them?

_____
_____
_____
_____
_____
_____
_____

The fact God remembers our suffering should be very comforting.
Read Revelation 21:4 and describe the intimacy God desires from you:

_____
_____
_____
_____
_____
_____
_____

"Record my misery; list my **tears**
on your scroll — are they not in your record?"

Psalm 56:8

FAITH TALK

Third Day

God's love is faithful - I will
drink it in, and then share it!

How will you share your faith today?
_____
_____
_____
_____
_____
_____
_____
_____

What is your favorite Bible verse? Why?
_____
_____
_____
_____
_____
_____
_____

*"From that time on Jesus began to explain to his disciples
that he must go to Jerusalem and suffer many things
at the hands of the elders, the chief priests and the teachers of
the law, and that he must be killed and on the*
third day *be raised to life."*

Matthew 16:21

Christian Life Coaching by LtA

Goes Before You

The Lord will lead me through
what He leads me into.

How do you feel when you step out in faith?

_____
_____
_____
_____
_____
_____
_____

Do you have to feel equipped and ready before you step out in faith?

_____
_____
_____
_____
_____
_____
_____
_____

*"The Lord your God, who is **going before you**, will fight for you, as he did for you in Egypt, before your very eyes"*

Deuteronomy 1:30

FAITH TALK

Anchor

Jesus penetrates my soul,
saturates my spirit,
is my Promised One!

How are you allowing the Holy Spirit access to your life? How does the guidance of the Holy Spirit work?

_____
_____
_____
_____
_____
_____
_____
_____

If you are not being transparent to the work of the Holy Spirit, how are you leading a meaningful and rewarding life in Christ?

_____
_____
_____
_____
_____
_____
_____
_____

*"We have this hope as an **anchor** for the soul,
firm and secure."*

Hebrews 6:19

I Seek You

God is the renewal of the strength
I need to make it through this
fast paced, stressful life.

How do you feel when you are trying to do life without the strength of the Lord?

_____
_____
_____
_____
_____
_____
_____
_____

What circumstances cause you to leave God out of the equation?

_____
_____
_____
_____
_____
_____
_____
_____

*"You, God, are my God, earnestly **I seek you**;*
I thirst for you, my whole being longs for you,
in a dry and parched land where there is no water.
² I have seen you in the sanctuary and beheld
your power and your glory.
³ Because your love is better than life, my lips will glorify you."

Psalm 63:1-3

FAITH TALK

Walk Humbly

I will do my best to treat people justly,
love mercy and walk
humbly with you Lord.

Will you take this pledge to treat people justly, love mercy and walk humbly with the Lord?

_____
_____
_____
_____
_____
_____
_____
_____
_____

List circumstances that would hinder your ability to keep this pledge:

_____
_____
_____
_____
_____
_____
_____
_____

*"He has shown you, O mortal, what is good.
And what does the LORD require of you?
To act justly and to love mercy
and to **walk humbly** with your God."*

Micah 6:8

Your Joy

God gives me the
promise of tomorrow.

What does it mean to you that tomorrow is a promise from God?

_____
_____
_____
_____
_____
_____
_____
_____
_____

List a few of God's other promises:

_____
_____
_____
_____
_____
_____
_____

*"So with you: Now is your time of grief,
but I will see you again and you will rejoice,
and no one will take away* **your joy**.*"*

John 16:22

FAITH TALK

Everything

God provides for my every need,
I do not need to be concerned
about my provisions.

Explain the comfort you feel by knowing that God provides for your every need:

_____
_____
_____
_____
_____
_____
_____
_____

Describe a time that the enemy had you doubting that God would sustain you:

_____
_____
_____
_____
_____
_____
_____
_____

"Everything that lives and moves about will be food for you.

Just as I gave you the green plants,
I now give you **everything**.*"*

Genesis 9:3

Freedom

I will give the gift of
freedom to others
just as I have been set free!

How will you give this gift of freedom to others?
_____
_____
_____
_____
_____
_____
_____
_____

List as many things as you can think of that Christ has set you free from:
_____
_____
_____
_____
_____
_____
_____
_____

"Recently you repented and did what is right in my sight: Each of you proclaimed **freedom** *to your own people. You even made a covenant before me in the house that bears my Name."*

Jeremiah 34:15

FAITH TALK

Lust and Pride

God is the standard setter in my life—
not people.

How is God setting the standards for your living? Give examples:

_____
_____
_____
_____
_____
_____
_____
_____

How do you respond to people that try to set your standards for you?

_____
_____
_____
_____
_____
_____
_____
_____

"For everything in the world—the lust of the flesh, the
lust of the eyes, and the pride of life
—comes not from the Father but from the world."

1 John 2:16

Perfecter of Faith

Like any muscle in my body my faith
is like a muscle I must
exercise to make it stronger.

Does your faith get expressed in how you use your resources?
___
___
___
___
___
___
___
___
___

How can you exercise your faith muscle?
___
___
___
___
___
___
___
___
___

"fixing our eyes on Jesus, the pioneer and
perfecter of faith.
*For the joy set before him he endured the cross,
scorning its shame, and sat down
at the right hand of the throne of God."*

Hebrews 12:2

FAITH TALK

Actions in Truth

I will slow down and focus less
on my earning so I can
see and meet the needs of others.

Are you actively on the lookout for meeting someone's needs?
___
___
___
___
___
___
___
___

Sometimes people are simply too proud to receive a grace gift offering. How do you respond to this person?
___
___
___
___
___
___
___
___

[17]" If anyone has material possessions and sees a brother or sister in need but has no pity on them, how can the love of God be in that person? [18] Dear children, let us not love with words or speech but with

actions and in truth."

1 John 3:17-18

Spirit of God

Worrying and anxiety are the barometer
of my faith - when I feel these
emotions, it will be my trigger to pray.

Is there any anger, jealousy, discontentment, regret, unforgiveness, worry or anxiety you need to let go of?

_____
_____
_____
_____
_____
_____
_____

Worry and anxiety reflects a lack of confidence in God and a tendency to take on burdens. Take this pledge: "I will stop and pray as soon as I feel ..."

_____
_____
_____
_____
_____
_____
_____
_____

*"For the **Spirit God gave** us does not make us timid, but gives us power, love and self-discipline."*

2 Timothy 1:7

FAITH TALK

Teach Us To Pray

My spirit life will take flight
through my prayer life.

How does your prayer life play a role in pursuing a faith that endures?

_____
_____
_____
_____
_____
_____
_____
_____
_____

How do you feel prior to praying and casting your cares? How do you feel after praying and casting your cares?

_____
_____
_____
_____
_____
_____
_____
_____
_____

*"One day Jesus was praying in a certain place.
When he finished, one of his disciples said to him,*

"'Lord, teach us to pray,

just as John taught his disciples.'"

Luke 11:1

Purified

I will stop finding faults about myself
and start honoring God
for the work He is doing in my life.

Why does being made in His image matter? Does our culture today delineate value and worth?

___
___
___
___
___
___
___
___
___
___

Describe how you are wonderfully made in His image:

___
___
___
___
___
___
___
___
___
___

"who gave himself for us to redeem *us from all wickedness and to* **purify** *for himself a people that are his very own, eager to do what is good."*

Titus 2:14

FAITH TALK

Tomorrow
I trust God with my tomorrow.

What do you have going on in your life that you need to trust God with?

_____
_____
_____
_____
_____
_____
_____
_____

There are three areas in which God's will can be revealed: His Word, the Holy Spirit's leading, and peace. If all three are in agreement, it is a good sign of God's leading and His will. Which specific aspect of your life are you seeking His will?

_____
_____
_____
_____
_____
_____
_____
_____

"Therefore do not worry about **tomorrow,**
for tomorrow will worry about itself.
Each day has enough trouble of its own."

Matthew 6:34

To Him Be The Glory

I do not have to know all the whys
and have all the answers,
I need to know the One who does.

How do you know that God is sovereign and omnipotent?

_____
_____
_____
_____
_____
_____
_____

Would it change your faith in Christ if you didn't feel this way?

_____
_____
_____
_____
_____
_____
_____

"But grow in the grace and knowledge
of our Lord and Savior Jesus Christ.
To him be glory
both now and forever! Amen."

2 Peter 3:18

FAITH TALK

All Things

I will take more time to listen to people
and learn who they are for the Gospel's sake.

Do you listen to respond with your two-cents, or do you listen with compassion to hear?

_____
_____
_____
_____
_____
_____
_____
_____

How do you feel when you are interrupted? When you are being rushed? When you know they aren't listening?

_____
_____
_____
_____
_____
_____
_____
_____

"To the weak I became weak, to win the weak.
*I have become **all things** to*
all people so that by all possible
means I might save some."

1 Corinthians 9:22

Full Light

My paths grow brighter everyday
as I walk in full light.

How are you walking in full light?

___
___
___
___
___
___
___
___

Describe any circumstances when the light is not as bright:

___
___
___
___
___
___
___
___

"The path of the righteous is
like the morning sun,
shining ever brighter till
the **full light** of day."
Proverbs 4:18

FAITH TALK

Life In His Name

When my heart is fully committed to Christ
is when I receive the benefits of the relationship.

Explain how your heart is committed to Christ:

___

What are the benefits you are receiving from your relationship with Jesus?

___

*"But these are written that you may
believe that Jesus is the Messiah,
the Son of God, and that by
believing you may have*

life in his name."

John 20:31

Motives

God is not obligated to perform to
my wishes but rather to act
according to His will.

When you pray, are your motives correct?
_____
_____
_____
_____
_____
_____
_____
_____
_____

When you pray in front of people, are you motives correct?
_____
_____
_____
_____
_____
_____
_____
_____
_____

*"When you ask, you do not receive,
because you ask with wrong*
motives, *that you may
spend what you get on your pleasures."*

James 4:3

FAITH TALK

Records

I will not keep records of how
people have mistreated me.

If you have been keeping records of wrongs against you, vow now to rip them up!

_____
_____
_____
_____
_____
_____
_____
_____

Explain how keeping these records may damage you and your relationships with the people on the record:

_____
_____
_____
_____
_____
_____
_____
_____

"It does not dishonor others, it is not self-seeking, it is not easily angered, it keeps no **record** *of wrongs."*

1 Corinthians 13:5

Strength

I am not called to walk in my own strength-
I am privileged to walk in His.

Describe an instance when you were aware of walking in God's strength:

_____
_____
_____
_____
_____
_____
_____
_____

Juxtapose by describing a time when you were aware you were not walking in God's strength:

_____
_____
_____
_____
_____
_____
_____
_____

32 "It is God who arms me with **strength**
and keeps my way secure.
33 He makes my feet like the feet of a deer; he causes
me to stand on the heights.
34 He trains my hands for battle; my arms can
bend a bow of bronze."

Psalm 18:32-34

FAITH TALK

With You

The Lord goes before me;
I am never alone.

How do you sense His presence in your life?

_____
_____
_____
_____
_____
_____
_____
_____
_____

Describe how you actively pursue God's presence each day:

_____
_____
_____
_____
_____
_____
_____
_____
_____

*"**The Lord** himself **goes before you** and will be
with you; he will never leave you nor forsake you.
Do not be afraid; do **not be discouraged.**"*

Deuteronomy 31:8

Working Out Salvation

Quoting scripture doesn't
make me a Christian;
working out my salvation does.

What does working out your salvation mean to you?

_____
_____
_____
_____
_____
_____
_____
_____
_____

How often do you work to bring your salvation to fruition? What are you doing when you are?

_____
_____
_____
_____
_____
_____
_____
_____
_____

"continue to work out your **salvation with fear and trembling**"

Philippians 2:12

FAITH TALK

Eternal Pleasures

I can go boldly to the throne because
I am confident of God's love for me.

Explain how you are confident of God's love for you:

___

How is His delight in you being demonstrated?

___

"*You make known to me the path of life;
you will fill me with joy in your presence,*
with ***eternal pleasures*** *at your right hand."*

Psalm 16:11

Works of Your Hands

The Lord will work out
His plan for my life.

Do you know God's plan for your life?
_____
_____
_____
_____
_____
_____
_____
_____
_____

Is He still revealing this plan to you?
_____
_____
_____
_____
_____
_____
_____
_____
_____

"The Lord will vindicate me;
your love, Lord, endures forever—
do not abandon the
works of your hands.*"*

Psalm 138:8

FAITH TALK

Patience and Love
Difficult people deserve
my patience and love.

Who are the difficult persons in your life right now to whom you need to show patience and love?

___

What are you doing so that your heart and mind might be renewed to handle undesirable situations?

___

"Love never fails."

1 Corinthians 13:8

Weary and Burdened

Cling to the One
who gives rest.

In what ways have you struggled to believe that God uses difficult circumstances for your good?

_____
_____
_____
_____
_____
_____
_____
_____
_____
_____

How are you clinging to Jesus? Is it only in uncomfortable situations or undesirable circumstances?

_____
_____
_____
_____
_____
_____
_____
_____

"Come to me, all you who are
weary and burdened,
and I will give you rest."
Matthew 11:28

FAITH TALK

Deliverance

Anticipate God's deliverance from
undesirable situations.

Has God taught you to respond to difficulties in different ways, so that you are trained by them?

_____
_____
_____
_____
_____
_____
_____
_____
_____

From which undesirable situation are you awaiting God's deliverance?

_____
_____
_____
_____
_____
_____
_____
_____
_____

"Moses answered the people, 'Do not be afraid.
Stand firm and you will see the **deliverance**
the Lord will bring you today. The Egyptians
you see today you will never see again.
14 The Lord will fight for you; you need only to be still.'"

Exodus 14:13-14

Royal Position
God, interrupt me and use me!

Do you allow interruptions in your life?

_____
_____
_____
_____
_____
_____
_____
_____
_____
_____

Delays, diversions, and distractions are interruptions that could be viewed as thieves taking away your peace, or they can be seen as divinely ordered construction zones that God adds to our lives. Describe a recent interruption in your life:

_____
_____
_____
_____
_____
_____
_____
_____
_____

"For if you remain silent at this time, relief and deliverance for the Jews will arise from another place, but you and your father's family will perish. And who knows but that you have come to your **royal position** for such a time as this?"

Esther 4:14

FAITH TALK

Enough For Us

If God is all I have,
I have all I desire.

Explain how you agree or disagree with the above statement:

Is there any area of your life in which you feel self-sufficient?

"Philip said, 'Lord, show us the
Father and that will be
enough for us.'"

John 14:8

Pardon Your Servant

I have no say in my family tree.
God uses who He calls
and it's not based on my pedigree.

Do you believe God is able to use whomever He chooses?

_____
_____
_____
_____
_____
_____
_____
_____

Which of the apostles do you most identify with? Why?

_____
_____
_____
_____
_____
_____
_____
_____

"Moses said to the Lord,
'Pardon your servant,
Lord. I have never been eloquent,
neither in the past nor since
you have spoken to your servant.
I am slow of speech and tongue.'"

Exodus 4:10

FAITH TALK

Write

The greatest and most important
pages of my story
have yet to be written.

How do you feel knowing that your story is still being written?

_____
_____
_____
_____
_____
_____
_____
_____
_____
_____

How are you participating in the storytelling? Is it being written in pen or pencil?

_____
_____
_____
_____
_____
_____
_____
_____
_____
_____

*"This is what the Lord, the God of Israel,
says: '**Write** in a book all the
words I have spoken to you.'"*

Jeremiah 30:2

Dwell In Your Hearts

The very same Power that
brought the Universe into being,
dwells in every believer.

What responsibility do you feel knowing that the Lord lives in you?

_____
_____
_____
_____
_____
_____
_____
_____
_____
_____

Describe on a regular basis how you take care of the temple in which the Holy Spirit dwells:

_____
_____
_____
_____
_____
_____
_____
_____
_____
_____

> *"I pray that out of his glorious riches he may strengthen you with power through his Spirit in your inner being, 17 so that Christ may* **dwell in your hearts** *through faith."*
> Ephesians 3:16-17

FAITH TALK

Forms the Hearts

I'm different from everyone else.
So, my relationship with
God will be unique as well.

How is your relationship with God different from others?

_____
_____
_____
_____
_____
_____
_____
_____
_____
_____

Do you ever find yourself jealous of other's perceived relationship with God?

_____
_____
_____
_____
_____
_____
_____
_____
_____
_____

"*he who* **forms the hearts**
*of all, who considers
everything they do."*

Psalm 33:15

Work of Your Hand

God is painting a picture of
my life. Though I may not see all of it
at once, it's a masterpiece to Him!

How much of the picture has God revealed to you so far?

_____
_____
_____
_____
_____
_____
_____
_____

Do you wish you had more or less of the picture? Why?

_____
_____
_____
_____
_____
_____
_____
_____

*"Yet you, Lord, are our Father.
We are the clay, you are the
potter; we are all the*
work of your hand.*"*

Isaiah 64:8

FAITH TALK

Wonderfully Made
I am valuable to God.

Explain how you are valuable to God:
_____
_____
_____
_____
_____
_____
_____
_____

In Luke 15 Jesus tells three stories. Explain how each story expresses your value to Christ:
_____
_____
_____
_____
_____
_____
_____
_____
_____

"I praise you because I am fearfully and
wonderfully made;
*your works are wonderful,
I know that full well."*

Psalm 139:14

Christian Life Coaching by LtA

Heart and Spirit
Inner purity = Outer power

What does inner purity and outer power have in common?

___
___
___
___
___
___
___
___

Has the condition of your heart changed over time through the leading of the Holy Spirit? How so?

___
___
___
___
___
___
___
___

*"Create in me a pure **heart**, O God,
and renew a steadfast
spirit within me."*

Psalm 51:10

FAITH TALK

Weakness Turned to Strength

I'm in the perfect position
for God to use me – imperfect.

How is your imperfection a good thing for God to use?

_____
_____
_____
_____
_____
_____
_____
_____

Ephesians 4 teaches the more we grow in Christ, the stronger and more unified we will be as a church. Describe how your growth is helping the church:

_____
_____
_____
_____
_____
_____
_____
_____

32 "And what more shall I say? I do not have time to tell about Gideon, Barak, Samson and Jephthah, about David and Samuel and the prophets, 33 who through faith conquered kingdoms, administered justice, and gained what was promised; who shut the mouths of lions, 34 quenched the fury of the flames, and escaped the edge of the sword; whose **weakness was turned to strength;** *and who became powerful in battle and routed foreign armies."*

Hebrews 11:32-34

Image: Bakhur Nick/Shutterstock.com

FAITH TALK

Missing the Mark- All Have Sinned

I won't get fit watching
someone exercise, or nourished
watching someone eat.

My relationship with Jesus will not grow through someone else's faith.
Are you growing in faith and knowledge? How?

_____
_____
_____
_____
_____
_____
_____
_____
_____
_____

List the character qualities in 2 Peter 3 that need to be added to your beginning point of faith in order for maturity to take place:

_____
_____
_____
_____
_____
_____
_____
_____

"for all have sinned and
fall short *of*
the glory of God"

Romans 3:23

Seek His Face

My faith doesn't keep
me from trouble,
it carries me through it.

How did your faith carry you through your last life storm?

_____
_____
_____
_____
_____
_____
_____
_____
_____

Faith in Christ is never misplaced. Luke and Mark tell the story of Jesus commanding the wind and water to obey Him. What do you think is the significance of Jesus calming the storm?

_____
_____
_____
_____
_____
_____
_____
_____

"Look to the Lord and his strength;
seek his face *always."*

1 Chronicles 16:11

FAITH TALK

New Birth

I will accept setbacks
without losing my trust in God.

Were you able to go through a setback and maintain your trust in God?

_____
_____
_____
_____
_____
_____
_____
_____

Why do you think it was important for Jesus to come into the world in a manger? Stay at the homes of whomever would welcome Him? Spend His last night before His crucifixion in a Garden?

_____
_____
_____
_____
_____
_____
_____
_____

"Praise be to the God and Father of our Lord Jesus Christ!
In his great mercy he has given us **new birth** *into a*
living hope through the resurrection of Jesus Christ from the dead"

1 Peter 1:3

Highly Esteemed
I will answer fear with faith.

Have you ever questioned why something was happening in your life that was unpleasant?

_____
_____
_____
_____
_____
_____
_____
_____
_____

Once the undesirable event passed, what was the lesson God revealed to you?

_____
_____
_____
_____
_____
_____
_____
_____
_____
_____

> *"'Do not be afraid, you who are* ***highly esteemed****,' he said. 'Peace! Be strong now; be strong.' When he spoke to me, I was strengthened and said 'Speak, my lord, since you have given me strength.'"*
>
> Daniel 10:19

FAITH TALK

I Called to You

When I was near burnout
You put new life in me.

How is God putting new life in you?

_____
_____
_____
_____
_____
_____
_____

There are no shortcuts. The only way to replace the sway of this world is to replace it with God's Truth; and the only infallible source of God's Truth is His revealed Word, the Bible. Describe the different ways you are exposing yourself to His Word on a daily and weekly basis:

_____
_____
_____
_____
_____
_____
_____
_____

"Lord my God, ***I called to you***
for help, and you healed me."

Psalm 30:2

Beyond Our Understanding

Whatever my heart's desire is -
nothing equals God.

I will seek God and be receptive to His voice.
Is there anyone in your life refusing God's voice? What reasons would you give to them to listen to Him?

_____
_____
_____
_____
_____
_____
_____
_____
_____

Do you seek His face or His hand more?

_____
_____
_____
_____
_____
_____
_____
_____

"God's voice thunders in marvelous ways; he does great things **beyond our understanding**. He says to the snow 'Fall on the earth,' and to the rain shower, 'Be a mighty downpour.'"

Job 37:5-6

FAITH TALK

There Is No Other

God is sovereign yesterday,
today and forever.

Do you ever doubt God's sovereignty? If so, what were the circumstances surrounding your doubt?

_____
_____
_____
_____
_____
_____
_____
_____

How would your life change if you couldn't trust that the One who says He loves you is fully able to act on that love in all ways?

_____
_____
_____
_____
_____
_____
_____

> [5] *"I am the Lord, and* **there is no other***;*
> *apart from me there is no God.*
> *I will strengthen you, though you have not acknowledged me,*
> [6] *so that from the rising of the sun to the place of its setting*
> *people may know there is none besides me.*
> *I am the Lord, and there is no other."*

Isaiah 45:5-6

Living Hope

*Lord, remind me
of Whose I am.*

Christians are questioning "Who am I" when the statement should be Whose I am!
Explain who you are in Christ:

___
___
___
___
___
___
___
___

*Ephesians 1, Colossians 3 and Hebrews 9 describe a believer's inheritance.
List your inheritance in Christ:*

___
___
___
___
___
___
___
___

*"Praise be to the God and Father of our Lord Jesus Christ!
In his great mercy he has given us new birth into a*

living hope *through the resurrection of Jesus Christ from the dead, ⁴ and into an inheritance that can never perish, spoil or fade. This inheritance is kept in heaven for you"*

1 Peter 1:3-4

FAITH TALK

Stewards of God's Grace

My life is a gift from God,
every breath a miracle.
He has given me gifts and talents to glorify Him,
I will be a good steward.

Believers have been given one or more spiritual gifts, none of us has them all.
What spiritual gifts has God given you?

_____
_____
_____
_____
_____
_____
_____
_____
_____

Are you frustrated when your spiritual gifts aren't recognized? Why?

_____
_____
_____
_____
_____
_____
_____
_____
_____

*"Each of you should use whatever gift you
have received to serve others, as faithful*
stewards of God's grace
in its various forms."

1 Peter 4:10

Christian Life Coaching by LtA

Take Heart
It won't be easy,
but it will be worth it.

What challenges have you faced as a believer in Christ?

_____
_____
_____
_____
_____
_____
_____
_____
_____

Have you ever waivered in your faith during these challenges? If so, explain:

_____
_____
_____
_____
_____
_____
_____
_____

"I have told you these things, so that in me you may have peace. In this world you will have trouble.
But **take heart**! *I have overcome the world."*

John 16:33

FAITH TALK

Seek First His Kingdom

God will answer what
I'm desperate for
when I am at my weakest.

Explain how God met your desperate need:

_____
_____
_____
_____
_____
_____
_____
_____
_____

Did this need get met just when you needed it, or did it take longer than you expected?

_____
_____
_____
_____
_____
_____
_____
_____
_____

"But seek first his **kingdom**
*and his righteousness, and all
these things will be given to you as well."*

Matthew 6:33

Satisfy
The Lord is the only
One who can satisfy my soul.

Explain how God has been the only One to satisfy your soul when others couldn't:

___
___
___
___
___
___
___
___
___
___

We begin with a decision to love God. That love grows as we gain knowledge and understanding of Who God is. List the characteristics of God that has helped you grow in your love for Him:

___
___
___
___
___
___
___
___
___
___

"As for me, I will be vindicated and will see your face;
when I awake, I will be **satisfied**
with seeing your likeness."

Psalm 17:15

FAITH TALK

Gift of the Holy Spirit

What I have in my life isn't important,
it's Who I have in
my life that matters most.

List all the people you love and admire and compare that to the love of God:

_____
_____
_____
_____
_____
_____
_____
_____
_____

Describe the different kinds of love you can experience during your journey with Christ:

_____
_____
_____
_____
_____
_____
_____
_____
_____

"Peter replied, 'Repent and be baptized,
every one of you, in the name
of Jesus Christ for the forgiveness
of your sins. And you will receive the
gift of the Holy Spirit'".

Acts 2:38

Give

Who is my neighbor-
anyone in need.

Neighbors are not subject to boundaries in a subdivision. *How can you reach out beyond your borders?*

_____
_____
_____
_____
_____
_____
_____
_____

When you reach out in love to those in need, is the compassion paired with evangelism?

_____
_____
_____
_____
_____
_____
_____
_____

*"**Give** to the one who asks you,
and do not turn away from the one
who wants to borrow from you."*

Matthew 5:42

FAITH TALK

Shield of Faith

I will starve any doubts
I have by feeding my faith.

How can you actively prepare to starve your doubts with faith?

_____
_____
_____
_____
_____
_____
_____
_____
_____

Can a mind that doubts ever be at peace? Explain:

_____
_____
_____
_____
_____
_____
_____

"In addition to all this, take up the
shield of faith,
*with which you can extinguish all the
flaming arrows of the evil one."*

Ephesians 6:16

I Will Help You

The process of waiting
strengthens my faith
in relying on the Supplier.

When were you in a time of waiting on God?

_____
_____
_____
_____
_____
_____
_____
_____

Did you ever doubt or fear that God would not sustain you?

_____
_____
_____
_____
_____
_____
_____
_____

*"For I am the Lord your God
who takes hold of your right hand
and says to you, Do not fear;*
I will help you."

Isaiah 41:13

FAITH TALK

Fully Committed

God's focus is on
how I turn out.

When did you realize God was more concerned about how committed you are to Him rather than your spiritual performance?

_____
_____
_____
_____
_____
_____
_____
_____
_____
_____

Why is it important that, on our journey with Christ, we become more like Him?

_____
_____
_____
_____
_____
_____
_____
_____
_____
_____

*"For the eyes of the Lord range throughout the earth to strengthen those whose hearts are **fully committed** to him."*

2 Chronicles 16:9

The Word doesn't Fail
Faith engages God,
fear engages the enemy.

When did you put the Word to the test?

_____
_____
_____
_____
_____
_____
_____
_____

When you speak scriptures over your circumstances and engage the power of God through prayer, does your fear lessen?

_____
_____
_____
_____
_____
_____
_____
_____

> *"For no word from God will ever fail."*
>
> Luke 1:37

FAITH TALK

Where You Go I Will Go

Small acts of love and kindness
can take up a big part
of someone's heart.

What was the last act of kindness you gave to someone?

_____
_____
_____
_____
_____
_____
_____
_____

By practicing kindness, you will lead a healthier, more fulfilling, selfless life.
Do you believe kindness is subjective? Why or why not?

_____
_____
_____
_____
_____
_____
_____
_____

"But Ruth replied, 'Don't urge me to leave you
or to turn back from you.
Where you go I will go,
and where you stay I will stay.
Your people will be my people and your God my God.'"

Ruth 1:16

By Faith

If God revealed everything to me,
I wouldn't need to live by faith.

God does give us revelation. What was the last revelation He gave you?

_____
_____
_____
_____
_____
_____
_____
_____

Did this revelation buoy your faith?

_____
_____
_____
_____
_____
_____
_____
_____

"**By faith** *we understand that the universe was formed at God's command, so that what is seen was not made out of what was visible.*"

Hebrews 11:3

FAITH TALK

Commands

Behavior and belief go
hand in hand.

Obeying Jesus is evidence I love Him.
Define what obedience in Christ means to you:

_____
_____
_____
_____
_____
_____
_____
_____
_____
_____

List the various environmental influences on your behavior:

_____
_____
_____
_____
_____
_____
_____
_____
_____
_____

"If you love me, keep

my **commands***."*

John 14:15

Christian Life Coaching by LtA

Gentle Whisper
God's silence is
not His absence.

I will wait and listen.

Have you ever felt that God's silence was His absence? Explain:

_____
_____
_____
_____
_____
_____
_____
_____

What do you do during the silent periods? Do you lean in to hear Him or do you find yourself wandering? Explain:

_____
_____
_____
_____
_____
_____
_____
_____

"*After the earthquake came a fire, but the Lord was not in the fire. And after the fire came a* **gentle whisper**."

1 Kings 19:12

FAITH TALK

Abyss

When the devil tries to condemn me
of my mistakes, I will rebuke him and
remind him of his future.

Have you ever taken a stand over the enemy?
_____
_____
_____
_____
_____
_____
_____
_____

Write down the scriptures you will use to speak against the enemy's attacks:
_____
_____
_____
_____
_____
_____

"And I saw an angel coming down out of heaven, having the key to the **Abyss** and holding in his hand a great chain. ² He seized the dragon, that ancient serpent, who is the devil, or Satan, and bound him for a thousand years. ³ He threw him into the Abyss, and locked and sealed it over him, to keep him from deceiving the nations anymore until the thousand years were ended. After that, he must be set free for a short time."

Revelation 20:1-3

God's Glory

The timing of God is for the glory of God.

Have you ever questioned God's timing?

_____
_____
_____
_____
_____
_____
_____
_____

What do you think God's perfect purpose was for putting you in a situation or allowing a situation to come into your life? What benefit came from it?

_____
_____
_____
_____
_____
_____
_____
_____

"When he heard this, Jesus said, 'This sickness will not end in death. No, it is for **God's glory** *so that God's Son may be glorified through it.'"*

John 11:4

FAITH TALK

Light and Salvation

If I increase my faith by
absorbing the Word of God,
my fears will be drowned out.

Are you facing any fears? What does this say about the condition of your heart?

_____
_____
_____
_____
_____
_____
_____
_____
_____

Describe the importance of the Truth in Scripture:

_____
_____
_____
_____
_____
_____
_____
_____

"The Lord is my **light and my salvation—**
whom shall I fear?
The Lord is the stronghold of my life—
of whom shall I be afraid?"

Psalm 27:1

Approaching God

My prayers make a difference
not because I say them
but because of Who hears them.

Do you have an active prayer life? Is your prayer life connected to your hope in Christ?

_____
_____
_____
_____
_____
_____
_____
_____
_____

Describe a recent prayer you saw answered:

_____
_____
_____
_____
_____
_____
_____
_____
_____

"This is the confidence we have in
approaching God:
*that if we ask anything according
to his will, he hears us."*

1 John 5:14

FAITH TALK

Heart of Flesh

It's my job to love people,
it's God's job to change them.

Have you tried to change people? How frustrated did you become?

_____
_____
_____
_____
_____
_____
_____
_____
_____

What are you leaving out of the equation when you attempt to change people?

_____
_____
_____
_____
_____
_____
_____
_____
_____

²⁶ *"I will give you a new heart and put a new spirit in you;
I will remove from you your heart of stone and give you a*
heart of flesh. ²⁷ *And I will put my Spirit
in you and move you to follow my decrees
and be careful to keep my laws."*

Ezekiel 36:26-27

Have Nothing To Do With What Is Evil

I am distinct from the world.
I am wholly devoted to God!

Define your worldview. Then explain if you feel alienated from people who aren't followers of Christ:

_____
_____
_____
_____
_____
_____
_____
_____
_____

How are you counterbalancing Kingdom and secular in your day to day?

_____
_____
_____
_____
_____
_____
_____
_____
_____

[3] *"I hate what faithless people do;*
I will have no part in it.
[4] *The perverse of heart shall be far from me;*
I will **have nothing to do with what is evil.**"

Psalm 101:3-4

FAITH TALK

Tablet of Your Heart

Virtues, Loyalty hopes,
perseveres and endures.

Explain how having favor in the eyes of God makes you feel:
_____
_____
_____
_____
_____
_____
_____
_____

Do you feel this favor when you have any unrepentant sin in your life?
_____
_____
_____
_____
_____
_____
_____
_____

3 *"Let love and faithfulness never leave you;
bind them around your neck,*
write them on the **tablet of your heart**.
*4 Then you will win favor and a good name
in the sight of God and man."*

Proverbs 3:3-4

Image: Thoom/Shutterstock.com

FAITH TALK

Familiar With All My Ways

God knows my name and
Needs - I trust Him and will
walk by faith not by sight.

Explain how you walk in faith:

_____
_____
_____
_____
_____
_____
_____
_____
_____
_____

Explain what spiritual sight is:

_____
_____
_____
_____
_____
_____
_____
_____
_____
_____

"You have searched me, Lord, and you know me.
2 You know when I sit and when I rise; you perceive my thoughts from afar.
3 You discern my going out and my lying down; you are
familiar with all my ways.
4 Before a word is on my tongue you, Lord, know it completely."

Psalm 139:1-4

New Creation

When my heart is in
sync with Christ
He is glorified.

How are you in sync with Christ?
_____
_____
_____
_____
_____
_____
_____
_____
_____

When you are out of sync with Christ, how is your life impacted?
_____
_____
_____
_____
_____
_____
_____
_____
_____

"Therefore, if anyone is in Christ,
the **new creation** *has come:*
The old has gone, the new is here!"

2 Corinthians 5:17

FAITH TALK

Given to Those Who Believe
Faith is the most powerful
force in the Kingdom of God.

What are you doing in your daily walk with God to strengthen your faith in Him?

Are you building your life around things that have eternal significance? Explain:

> "But Scripture has locked up
> everything under the control of sin,
> so that what was promised,
> being given through faith in
> Jesus Christ, might be
> **given to those
> who believe.**"

Galatians 3:22

Spring of Living Water

Christians release the
rivers of God life and
love all over the world.

How are you releasing God's life to those around you?

_____
_____
_____
_____
_____
_____
_____
_____
_____

If you have been rejected by someone because of your faith, describe the circumstances and how it impacted your sharing the Gospel afterward:

_____
_____
_____
_____
_____
_____
_____
_____

"Lord, you are the hope of Israel;
all who forsake you will be put to shame.
Those who turn away from you will be written in the dust
because they have forsaken the Lord, the
spring of living water."

Jeremiah 17:13

FAITH TALK

Reverential Fear

If I fear God,
then I won't fear people.

Have you been fearful of people before placing your faith in Christ?

_____
_____
_____
_____
_____
_____
_____
_____

Has this fear of people changed in your Christian Life?

_____
_____
_____
_____
_____
_____
_____

"Do not be afraid of those who kill the body but cannot kill the soul. Rather, **be afraid of the One who can destroy both soul and body** *in hell."*

Matthew 10:28

Restore

I will choose words and the tone
I speak in to reflect love
like the rejuvenating rain
showers that produce new growth.

Have you been hurt by the sins of others? Did they know how their sins affected you?
___
___
___
___
___
___
___
___

Are you mindful that the words and the tone you speak in are a reflection of Jesus?
___
___
___
___
___
___
___
___
___

"Brothers and sisters, if someone is caught in a sin, you who live by the Spirit should **restore** that person gently. But watch yourselves, or you also may be tempted."

Galatians 6:1

FAITH TALK

Love is a Verb

When I show love toward someone
no matter how big or small the gesture,
I am showing my love toward God.

This love is what makes life so wonderful.
When you meet a need, are you accepting the praise or do you give all praise to God?

_____
_____
_____
_____
_____
_____
_____

How do you balance being gracious to the praise without accepting it?

_____
_____
_____
_____
_____
_____
_____

[19] "**We love because he first loved us.**
[20] Whoever claims to love God yet hates a brother or sister is a liar. For whoever does not love their brother and sister, whom they have seen, cannot love God, whom they have not seen.
[21] And he has given us this command: Anyone who loves God must also love their brother and sister."

1 John 4:19-21

A Fire In My Bones

I might be the reason someone
will read the Bible.

I pray that my life speaks louder than my lips.
Are you aware of your responsibility as an ambassador to Christ?

_____
_____
_____
_____
_____
_____
_____
_____
_____
_____

Explain what your responsibilities to the advancement of the Gospel means to you:

_____
_____
_____
_____
_____
_____
_____
_____
_____

"But if I say, 'I will not mention his word or speak anymore in his name,' his word is in my heart like a fire, a **fire shut up in my bones**. *I am weary of holding it in; indeed, I cannot."*

Jeremiah 20:9

FAITH TALK

My Heart Rejoices

As long as I have breath in my lungs,
I can be assured that God has a plan,
purpose and destiny for my life.

Do believe God has a plan, purpose and destiny for your life?

_____
_____
_____
_____
_____
_____
_____
_____
_____
_____

Are you living in the fullness of His plan for your life? Are you anxious about the future?

_____
_____
_____
_____
_____
_____
_____
_____
_____
_____

⁵ "But I trust in your unfailing love;
my heart rejoices *in your salvation.*
⁶ I will sing the Lord's praise, for he has been good to me."

Psalm 13:5-6

Everlasting Sign

God specializes in turning my ashes into beauty,
my failures into His successes.
He is big enough and I will trust His process.

Have you let go of your ashes? Make a list of the ashes you need to release:

___
___
___
___
___
___
___
___
___
___

He can't use the ashes if you retain them; pledge to let them go:

___
___
___
___
___
___
___
___
___
___

*"Instead of the thornbush will grow the juniper,
and instead of briers the myrtle will grow.
This will be for the Lord's renown,*
for an **everlasting sign**,
that will endure forever."

Isaiah 55:13

FAITH TALK

Light Shines

I will enter into God's presence
with devotion and He will enter
my life with His ruling power!

How are you showing devotion to the Lord?

_____
_____
_____
_____
_____
_____
_____
_____
_____

Luke 10 shows Martha and Mary as both devoted to the Lord but only one is praised for showing the proper devotion. Why?

_____
_____
_____
_____
_____
_____
_____
_____

"The **light shines** in the darkness,
and the darkness has not overcome it."

John 1:5

Greater Than The One Who Is In The World

Temptation is an opportunity
for me to stand tall.

Do the temptations Jesus endured affect the way you go through your encounters?

_____
_____
_____
_____
_____
_____
_____
_____
_____

What was your recent temptation? How did God guide you through it?

_____
_____
_____
_____
_____
_____
_____
_____

"You, dear children, are from God and have overcome them, because the one who is in you is **greater than the one who is in the world**.*"*

1 John 4:4

FAITH TALK

Give Without Sparing
Giving should be done without condition.

I will bless without strings attached.
Have you ever given and expected something in return?

_____
_____
_____
_____
_____
_____
_____
_____

Have you ever received a gift and the person giving it expected it to be used a certain way? How did this make you feel?

_____
_____
_____
_____
_____
_____
_____
_____

"All day long he craves for more, but the righteous **give without sparing**.*"*

Proverbs 21:26

Sacrifice

I will sacrifice something precious;
I'm not losing something - but passing it on.
I will let God's love flow through me.

What have you sacrificed in order to show God's love?

_____
_____
_____
_____
_____
_____
_____
_____

Why is it important for Christians to show sacrificial love?

_____
_____
_____
_____
_____
_____
_____
_____

"And do not forget to do good and to share with others, for with such **sacrifices** *God is pleased."*

Hebrews 13:16

FAITH TALK

Refresh Others
Kindness never
goes out of style.

Are you kinder than necessary?

Has a bad day ever turned into a better day when someone showed you kindness?

²⁴ *"One person gives freely, yet gains even more;*
another withholds unduly, but comes to poverty.
²⁵ *A generous person will prosper;*
whoever **refreshes others**
will be refreshed."

Proverbs 11:24-25

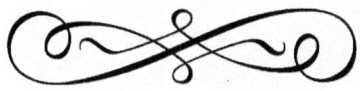

Serve

I will approach relationships from
a platform of being a servant, and
love without expecting love in return.

How do you approach your present relationships?

_____
_____
_____
_____
_____
_____
_____
_____

Do you have a person in your life who wears you out with their demands on your time? How are you responding to this person?

_____
_____
_____
_____
_____
_____
_____
_____
_____
_____

*"For even the Son of Man did not come
to be **served**, but to serve, and
to give his life as a ransom for many."*

Mark 10:45

FAITH TALK

Living in Peace & Holiness

When I feel God's peace,
I know I am in His will.

Have you felt peace in His will?

_____
_____
_____
_____
_____
_____
_____
_____

Have you ever felt like you are out of His will? Describe the contrast:

_____
_____
_____
_____
_____
_____
_____
_____

"Make every effort to **live in peace** *with everyone and to be holy;* *without* **holiness** *no one will see the Lord."*

Hebrews 12:14

Footstool

I can stand before people
because I bow only to the Lord.

Are you able to stand before people?

_____
_____
_____
_____
_____
_____
_____
_____
_____
_____

How are you bowing to the Lord?

_____
_____
_____
_____
_____
_____
_____
_____
_____
_____

*"To which of the angels did God ever say,
'Sit at my right hand
until I make your enemies a
footstool for your feet'"*

Hebrews 1:13

FAITH TALK

Light of Light

I will keep my eye
on the Son so I will grow.

Has your eye ever wandered away from the Lord?

_____
_____
_____
_____
_____
_____
_____
_____
_____
_____

What brought you back?

_____
_____
_____
_____
_____
_____
_____
_____

"When Jesus spoke again to the people, he said, 'I am the light of the world. Whoever follows me will never walk in darkness, but will have the **light of life**.*'"*

John 8:12

Christian Life Coaching by LtA

Image: Thoom/Shutterstock.com

FAITH TALK

Shelter

God shelters my heart and gives me
peace and strength each day.

How are you feeling God's strength?

_____
_____
_____
_____
_____
_____
_____
_____

Describe the peace of the Lord:

_____
_____
_____
_____
_____
_____
_____
_____

"For in the day of trouble he will keep me safe in his dwelling;
*he will hide me in the **shelter** of his sacred tent*
and set me high upon a rock."

Psalm 27:5

God Chooses

God's tool chest has very
interesting things in it.

He uses what the world discards and rejects in mighty ways.
Describe how God is using you in mighty ways:

_____
_____
_____
_____
_____
_____
_____
_____
_____
_____
_____

If God only used the powerful, would it diminish His Word?

_____
_____
_____
_____
_____
_____
_____

[27] "But **God chose** the foolish things of the world to shame the wise; God chose the weak things of the world to shame the strong. [28] God chose the lowly things of this world and the despised things—and the things that are not—to nullify the things that are"

1 Corinthians 1:27-28

FAITH TALK

My Yoke

When I stumble,
when I'm weakened,
when I miss the mark,
when I lack faith,
God provides the answers!

What answers has God provided to you?

_____
_____
_____
_____
_____
_____
_____
_____

Does God understand when you grow weary?

_____
_____
_____
_____
_____
_____
_____
_____

[29] *"Take my yoke upon you and learn from me,
for I am gentle and humble in heart, and you
will find rest for your souls.*
[30] *For **my yoke** is easy and my burden is light."*

Matthew 11:29-30

I Am With You
I am never alone!

Do you feel God with you? Why or why not?

_____
_____
_____
_____
_____
_____
_____
_____
_____

What Word from the Lord would encourage you, that you are not alone?

_____
_____
_____
_____
_____
_____
_____
_____

> *'Be strong, all you people of the land, declares the Lord, 'and work.*
> For **I am with you**,'
> *declares the Lord Almighty."*
>
> Haggai 2:4

FAITH TALK

Pruning

God is my master gardener.
He prunes - so I bloom.

Do you allow God to tend to your gardening needs?

_____
_____
_____
_____
_____
_____
_____
_____
_____

If you need to let something go and God has been dealing with you about it, write it down now and vow to trust the Lord to prune away what needs to go:

_____
_____
_____
_____
_____
_____
_____
_____
_____

*"He cuts off every branch in me
that bears no fruit, while every
branch that does bear fruit he* **prunes**
so that it will be even more fruitful."

John 15:2

Christian Life Coaching by LtA

Engraved
I am one of a kind masterpiece
and I will fulfill my destiny.

How are you God's masterpiece?
___
___
___
___
___
___
___
___

God knows your ways...and He knows them continually. Exercising our freedom against God's plan can be painful as illustrated by Saul/Paul. Is there any area of your life that you are resisting God?
___
___
___
___
___
___
___
___

"See, I have **engraved** you on
the palms of my hands;
your walls are ever before me."

Isaiah 49:16

FAITH TALK

Comforted

Let my heart be sensitive to
the things that move God's heart.

How can you become more sensitive to God's heart?

_____
_____
_____
_____
_____
_____
_____
_____

When we are born again, God gives us a new heart. The power of the Holy Spirit changes our hearts from sin-focused to God-focused. We do not become perfect - we still have our sinful flesh and the freedom to choose whether or not to obey it. Is there still an area of your life you need to address in order to become more God-focused?

_____
_____
_____
_____
_____
_____
_____
_____

"Blessed are those who mourn,
for they will be ***comforted.****"*

Matthew 5:4

Through Me
God is in control
and Jesus is still the answer.

Explain how you feel about knowing that you have the answer.

_____
_____
_____
_____
_____
_____
_____
_____
_____

Describe the difference between knowing you have the answer now, and before you had the answer. Is there more peace in your heart? Are your relationships better, etc.?

_____
_____
_____
_____
_____
_____
_____
_____
_____
_____

"Jesus answered, 'I am the way and the truth and the life.
*No one comes to the Father except **through me**.'"*

John 14:6

FAITH TALK

My Disciples

Since I am responsible
for my conduct,
I choose to love.

The only thing you can control is how you respond to life.
How do you choose to conduct yourself?

_____
_____
_____
_____
_____
_____
_____
_____
_____
_____

While going about your day-to-day, is it obvious that you are different from this world? Explain:

_____
_____
_____
_____
_____
_____
_____
_____
_____
_____

"By this everyone will know that you are **my disciples**, *if you love one another."*

John 13:35

His Love For Us

God loves me purely,
I trust Him completely.

How does God love you purely?
_____
_____
_____
_____
_____
_____
_____
_____
_____

Contrast how a "strings attached" love compares to Godly love:
_____
_____
_____
_____
_____
_____
_____
_____
_____

"But God demonstrates
his own love for us
in this: While we were still sinners,
Christ died for us."

Romans 5:8

FAITH TALK

Born of God

I will not rely on someone else's
relationship with Jesus to transform me.

I have the privilege to know Him. Peter emphasizes relationship between knowledge and godliness.

Explain the role knowledge plays in your ongoing spiritual transformation:

___

Are you actively pursuing a deeper relationship with God? If not, why not?

___

12 *"Yet to all who did receive him, to those who believed in his name, he gave the right to become children of God— 13 children born not of natural descent, nor of human decision or a husband's will,* **but born of God.**"

John 1:12-13

Blood of Jesus

I have the Spirit of a warrior;
the blood of the King flows through my veins;
the Greater Power lives in me;
I will walk in His power!

Explain the power of the blood of Jesus:

_____
_____
_____
_____
_____
_____
_____
_____
_____
_____

How do you exercise this power in your daily walk with Christ?

_____
_____
_____
_____
_____
_____
_____
_____
_____
_____

[19] "Therefore, brothers and sisters, since we have confidence to enter the Most Holy Place by the **blood of Jesus**, [20] by a new and living way opened for us through the curtain, that is, his body, [21] and since we have a great priest over the house of God"

Hebrews 10:19-21

FAITH TALK

Sprinkled With His Blood

I have Christ-like character
being developed in me.

I choose to know Him in the power of His resurrection.
What Christ-like character has been developed in you?

_____
_____
_____
_____
_____
_____
_____
_____
_____
_____

What does the power of the resurrection mean to you?

_____
_____
_____
_____
_____
_____
_____
_____

*"who have been chosen according to the foreknowledge
of God the Father, through the sanctifying work of the
Spirit, to be obedient to Jesus Christ and*

sprinkled with his blood:
Grace and peace be yours in abundance."

1 Peter 1:2

Christian Life Coaching by LtA

Water From The Sanctuary Flows

I am a channel, not a reservoir; I am called to outreach, not in-reach.

Are you only associating with saved people?

_____
_____
_____
_____
_____
_____
_____
_____

What outreach programs are you associated with? What outreach do you show in your faith journey?

_____
_____
_____
_____
_____
_____
_____
_____

"Fruit trees of all kinds will grow on both banks of the river. Their leaves will not wither, nor will their fruit fail. Every month they will bear fruit, because the

water from the sanctuary flows

to them. Their fruit will serve for food and their leaves for healing."

Ezekiel 47:12

FAITH TALK

You Know Me

The Lord gives me exactly
what I need when I need it.

Do you believe the Lord knows what you need and when you need it?

_____
_____
_____
_____
_____
_____
_____
_____

Has God used you to meet someone's needs? Describe:

_____
_____
_____
_____
_____
_____
_____

"You have searched me, Lord,
*and **you know me**."*

Psalm 139:1

Renewal by the Holy Spirit

God alone provides the renewal
of strength I need to make it
through this fast-paced, stressful life.

How are you allowing the Lord to renew your strength?

___
___
___
___
___
___
___
___
___

In what ways are you participating in the Lord's renewal of your strength?

___
___
___
___
___
___
___
___

*"he saved us, not because of righteous things we
had done, but because of his mercy. He saved us
through the washing of rebirth and*
renewal by the Holy Spirit"

Titus 3:5

Faith Is...

God doesn't give me the
whole picture so I will
put my trust in Him.

What promises of God do you need to review to have more confidence?

_____
_____
_____
_____
_____
_____
_____
_____
_____

Do you feel blessed or stressed to not have the whole picture?

_____
_____
_____
_____
_____
_____
_____
_____
_____

*"Now **faith is** confidence in
what we hope for and assurance
about what we do not see."*

Hebrews 11:1

Christian Life Coaching by LtA

In His Hand

I don't know what my
future holds but I know the
One who holds my future.

Explain why you are excited about your future:
_____
_____
_____
_____
_____
_____
_____
_____

How did you think about your future before you were born again?
_____
_____
_____
_____
_____
_____
_____
_____

"**In his hand** is the life of
every creature and
the breath of all mankind."

Job 12:10

FAITH TALK

Proclaim Freedom for the Captives

My prison doors are open. I don't have to live in bondage anymore. I will let God reveal His Truth.

Have you become unknowingly enslaved to something? Contrast freedom and slavery:

_____
_____
_____
_____
_____
_____
_____
_____

When did you realize your prison doors were opened by the Lord?

_____
_____
_____
_____
_____
_____
_____
_____

"The Spirit of the Sovereign Lord is on me,
because the Lord has anointed me
to proclaim good news to the poor.
He has sent me to bind up the brokenhearted,

to **proclaim freedom for the captives**
and release from darkness for the prisoners"

Isaiah 61:1

Honeycomb

Gracious words will echo throughout the person's day
To whom I spoke them.

How do you feel when you know you have made a person's day?

_____
_____
_____
_____
_____
_____
_____
_____

How do you feel when someone reaches out to you with no ulterior motives except to make your day a little brighter?

_____
_____
_____
_____
_____
_____
_____
_____

"Gracious words are a **honeycomb**, sweet to the soul and healing to the bones."

Proverbs 16:24

FAITH TALK

Raised Up On The Last Day

My seeking heart is evidence
that God is sovereignly
drawing me to Him.

How do you seek God daily?

_____
_____
_____
_____
_____
_____
_____
_____
_____
_____

How is God drawing you nearer to Him?

_____
_____
_____
_____
_____
_____
_____
_____
_____
_____

*"No one can come to me unless the Father
who sent me draws them, and I will*
raise them up at the last day."

John 6:44

Peacemaker

Christians are called to be
Peacemakers, not peacekeepers.

Explain the difference between peacemaking and peacekeeping:

_____
_____
_____
_____
_____
_____
_____
_____

Describe a recent peacekeeping attempt and its outcome. Is it a lasting peace?

_____
_____
_____
_____
_____
_____
_____
_____

"Blessed are the **peacemakers***,
for they will be called children of God."*

Matthew 5:9

FAITH TALK

Merciful

Choose to remember the good
things about people and events,
so the root of bitterness and
discontentment may not grow.

The devil roams about trying to gain a foothold. How are you actively thwarting his advances?

_____
_____
_____
_____
_____
_____
_____
_____
_____

List any known footholds the enemy has on you and vow to take that foothold back and give it to Jesus:

_____
_____
_____
_____
_____
_____
_____
_____
_____

"Blessed are the **merciful***,
for they will be shown mercy."*

Matthew 5:7

Peace

If I'm confused, anxious, worried, angry etc., that is evidence that I am not operating in faith.

As a believer I have been given His peace.
Explain how His peace blocks out anxiety, confusion, worry, anger etc.

___
___
___
___
___
___
___
___

If Jesus left you His peace, how can you be living more abundantly in that peace?

___
___
___
___
___
___
___
___

*"Peace I leave with you; my **peace** I give you. I do not give to you as the world gives. Do not let your hearts be troubled and do not be afraid."*

John 14:27

FAITH TALK

The Lord's Coming

I will wait expectantly on
God to work in my life.

How good are you at waiting?

Why does God teach us the value of the virtue of patience? What does patience look like? What does impatience look like?

"Be patient, then, brothers and sisters, until
the Lord's coming. See how the
farmer waits for the land to yield its valuable crop,
patiently waiting for the autumn and spring rains.
8 You too, be patient and stand firm,
because the Lord's coming is near."

James 5:7-8

Walk Together

*When I am blessed with friendships,
I won't take those
relationships for granted.*

Friendship is an opportunity for God to love them through me.
What kind of friend are you?

_____
_____
_____
_____
_____
_____
_____
_____
_____

Do you make friends easily? Are you on the lookout for someone who could use a friend?

_____
_____
_____
_____
_____
_____
_____
_____

"Do two **walk together**
unless they have agreed to do so?"

Amos 3:3

FAITH TALK

Built Up

I will never diminish myself
when I praise another.

The church has great potential for being a caring and healing community. *How are you building up the church?*

_____
_____
_____
_____
_____
_____
_____
_____
_____

Our flesh enjoys being praised. As long as it is not being exalted above God, are you offering praise to build someone up that might be struggling?

_____
_____
_____
_____
_____
_____
_____
_____
_____
_____

*"What then shall we say, brothers and sisters?
When you come together, each of you has a hymn,
or a word of instruction, a revelation,
a tongue or an interpretation. Everything must be
done so that the church may be* **built up**.*"*

1 Corinthians 14:26

A Good Measure

My thoughts, words, actions
are seeds I'm sowing.
By sowing kindness, mercy, and love, I'm investing in a good harvest.
What does your harvest look like?

_____
_____
_____
_____
_____
_____
_____
_____
_____
_____

Can you help others build their harvest?

_____
_____
_____
_____
_____
_____
_____
_____
_____

"Give, and it will be given to you.
A good measure, *pressed down,*
shaken together and running over,
will be poured into your lap. For with the measure
you use, it will be measured to you."

Luke 6:38

FAITH TALK

Scale a Wall

Sometimes my only mode of
transportation is a leap of faith.

How far can you jump? Describe the last leap of faith you took:

_____
_____
_____
_____
_____
_____
_____
_____

If God asked you to, would you follow Abram's example and leave everything behind that you have ever known to begin anew?

_____
_____
_____
_____
_____
_____
_____
_____
_____

*"With your help I can advance against a troop;
with my God I can* **scale a wall**.*"*

Psalm 18:29

Christian Life Coaching by LtA

Floodgates of Heaven

When I'm feeling helpless,
I will help someone.

How do you break the cycle of helplessness?

_____
_____
_____
_____
_____
_____
_____
_____

When you feel helpless, could God be asking you to reach out and help someone in need?

_____
_____
_____
_____
_____
_____
_____
_____

*"Bring the whole tithe into the storehouse,
that there may be food in my house.
Test me in this, says the Lord Almighty,
and see if I will not throw open the*

floodgates of heaven

*and pour out so much blessing that there
will not be room enough to store it."*

Malachi 3:10

FAITH TALK

He Delivered Me

Faith and giving into fear
do not intersect.

When faith is exercised, fear is transcended.
How should our fear impact our faith? How should our faith impact our fear?

_____
_____
_____
_____
_____
_____
_____
_____
_____
_____
_____

How would you help someone transcend from fear into faith in Jesus?

_____
_____
_____
_____
_____
_____
_____
_____
_____
_____

"I sought the Lord, and he answered me;
he delivered me *from all my fears."*

Psalm 34:4

Our Conscience Testifies

I will be the beauty amidst
worldly struggles.

Someone might encounter God for the first time through me.
How aware are you that you are a living testimony to God's saving grace?

_____
_____
_____
_____
_____
_____
_____
_____
_____

When was the last time you paused to reflect on how you are affecting your surroundings?

_____
_____
_____
_____
_____
_____
_____
_____
_____

"Now this is our boast:
Our conscience testifies
*that we have conducted ourselves in the world,
and especially in our relations with you,
with integrity and godly sincerity.
We have done so, relying not on worldly
wisdom but on God's grace."*

2 Corinthians 1:12

FAITH TALK

Enriched in Every Way

Grow spiritual muscles by
enriching someone else's life.

Are you on the lookout to enrich someone's life with the Gospel?

_____
_____
_____
_____
_____
_____
_____
_____

Muscles atrophy if not used. List the ways you can help grow the Kingdom in your day-to-day life:

_____
_____
_____
_____
_____
_____
_____
_____

"You will be **enriched in every way**
*so that you can be generous on every
occasion, and through us
your generosity will result
in thanksgiving to God."*

2 Corinthians 9:11

Sacrifice

I am willing to sacrifice who
I am now for the fullness of
who God intends me to become.

What does it mean to you to sacrifice who you are now?

_____
_____
_____
_____
_____
_____
_____
_____
_____

Do you feel it is necessary to make this sacrifice in order to become Christ-like?

_____
_____
_____
_____
_____
_____
_____
_____
_____

*"Therefore, I urge you, brothers and sisters, in view of God's mercy, to offer your bodies as a living **sacrifice**, holy and pleasing to God—this is your true and proper worship."*

Romans 12:1

FAITH TALK

Inheritance

I worship an omnipotent God.
My future is in His loving capable hands.
So I will dream BIG!

What does dreaming big mean to you?

_____
_____
_____
_____
_____
_____
_____
_____

If your big dream doesn't look like God's plan for your life, will you be disappointed?

_____
_____
_____
_____
_____
_____
_____
_____

*"Ask me, and I will make the nations your **inheritance**, the ends of the earth your possession."*

Psalm 2:8

Secure

Expecting life to be worth living can be discouraging if I'm not actively making it worth living.

What steps can you take to actively make life worth living?

_____
_____
_____
_____
_____
_____
_____
_____
_____

Job's life is proof that we don't always know what God is doing behind the scenes in our lives. Is there any area of your life that you haven't submitted to God's will?

_____
_____
_____
_____
_____
_____
_____
_____
_____

*"You will be **secure**, because there is hope;
you will look about you and take your rest in safety."*

Job 11:18

FAITH TALK

Not Seen And Yet Have Believed

Trusting in the Lord
means there will
be unanswered questions.

How well do you handle not having the answers?

_____
_____
_____
_____
_____
_____
_____
_____
_____
_____

How would your faith be affected if you did have all the answers?

_____
_____
_____
_____
_____
_____
_____
_____
_____
_____

"Then Jesus told him, 'Because you have
seen me, you have believed;
blessed are those who have
not seen and yet have believed.'"

John 20:29

My Strength & My Shield

Faith is belief without reservation.
I will live with bold confident faith.

Explain what believing without reservation means to you:

_____
_____
_____
_____
_____
_____
_____
_____

How is your faith an encouragement to the people in your life?

_____
_____
_____
_____
_____
_____
_____
_____
_____

"The Lord is **my strength and my shield**;
my heart trusts in him, and he helps me.
My heart leaps for joy,
and with my song I praise him."

Psalm 28:7

FAITH TALK

You Rule

I can pray confidently to God
because He Rules over all nations.

What does confident prayer sound like?

_____
_____
_____
_____
_____
_____
_____
_____
_____

Write a confident prayer over the leaders of the nations and this world:

_____
_____
_____
_____
_____
_____
_____
_____
_____
_____

"And said: 'Lord, the God of our ancestors, are you not the God who is in heaven? ***You rule*** *over all the kingdoms of the nations. Power and might are in your hand, and no one can withstand you.'"*

2 Chronicles 20:6

Forgiveness and Grace

In a world that demands justice, we can only truly understand the beauty of God's grace when we understand His love towards us. Once we grasp the magnitude of His love and the reality of the grace we have been shown, then forgiveness becomes an essential component of our journey with Christ. Jesus commanded us to forgive or our fellowship with God is hindered. It is not negotiable. "For if you forgive other people when they sin against you, your heavenly Father will also forgive you. 15 But if you do not forgive others their sins, your Father will not forgive your sins" Matthew 6:14-15. If forgiveness is that important for Jesus to command us to forgive, we should take time to look at how forgiveness and grace intertwine.

Praying this section will make you want to forgive quickly and rest in His endless grace.

Image : Vladis Chern/Shutterstock.com

FAITH TALK

Unveiled

First grace saves us;
then grace changes us through
submission to the leadership
of the best change agent - the Holy Spirit.

A characteristic of a Christian is exhibiting a completely unveiled openness before God, which allows our life to become a mirror for others.
Are you mirroring the Lord's own character? If yes, how so?

_____
_____
_____
_____
_____
_____
_____
_____

An important rule for us is to concentrate on keeping our lives open to God. Denial is quite powerful. If there is no felt need to change, then can change occur? Describe submitting to the leadership of the Holy Spirit. How has this submission changed your life? Your relationships?

_____
_____
_____
_____
_____
_____
_____
_____

*"And we all, who with **unveiled** faces contemplate the Lord's glory, are being transformed into his image with ever-increasing glory, which comes from the Lord, who is the Spirit."*

2 Corinthians 3:18

Christian Life Coaching by LtA

Alive In The Spirit

"You are worth the life of My Son."
This is my worth and value.

Do you minimize being declared righteous? Why or why not?

_____
_____
_____
_____
_____
_____
_____
_____
_____
_____

How does Jesus' sacrifice make you feel?

_____
_____
_____
_____
_____
_____
_____
_____
_____
_____

*"For Christ also suffered once for sins,
the righteous for the unrighteous,
to bring you to God.
He was put to death in the body
but made* **alive in the Spirit**.*"*

1 Peter 3:18

FAITH TALK

Save Not Condemn

Jesus gives grace
not disgrace.

The One with power to condemn me doesn't.
When you judge the person and not the sin, how does that make you feel?

_____
_____
_____
_____
_____
_____
_____
_____
_____

When you miss the mark, do people judge you? How does that make you feel?

_____
_____
_____
_____
_____
_____
_____
_____
_____

*"For God did not send his Son
into the world to condemn the world,*

but to **save** *the world through him."*

John 3:17

Broken Spirit

Only in the Kingdom
of God are broken
things of great value.

Did God have to break you in order to fill you with Himself?

_____
_____
_____
_____
_____
_____
_____
_____
_____
_____

In what ways were you rebelling against God that caused this breaking to become necessary?

_____
_____
_____
_____
_____
_____
_____
_____
_____
_____

*"My sacrifice, O God, is a **broken spirit**;
a broken and contrite heart you, God, will not despise."*

Psalm 51:17

FAITH TALK

Incomparable Riches of His Grace

*I am a trophy
of God's grace.*

What kind of trophy do you look like?

_____
_____
_____
_____
_____
_____
_____
_____
_____

What would more of God's favor in your life look like?

_____
_____
_____
_____
_____
_____
_____
_____
_____

[4] *"But because of his great love for us, God, who is rich in mercy,* [5] *made us alive with Christ even when we were dead in transgressions—it is by grace you have been saved.* [6] *And God raised us up with Christ and seated us with him in the heavenly realms in Christ Jesus,* [7] *in order that in the coming ages he might show the* **incomparable riches of his grace**, *expressed in his kindness to us in Christ Jesus."*

Ephesians 2:4-7

The Thief

The voice that tells me
I'm not good enough
is a liar!

What has God done to help you hear His voice? How are you listening to His voice?

_____
_____
_____
_____
_____
_____
_____
_____
_____

Satan, our great accuser, is a liar. Are you still listening to Satan's lies?

_____
_____
_____
_____
_____
_____
_____
_____
_____

*"**The thief** comes only to steal and kill and destroy; I have come that they may have life, and have it to the full."*

John 10:10

FAITH TALK

Strengthen & Protect

Protected in His love;
absorbed in His mercy;
breathing in His grace.

Explain how you breathe in God's grace:

_____
_____
_____
_____
_____
_____
_____
_____
_____

Describe your gratitude that God bestows His grace on you:

_____
_____
_____
_____
_____
_____
_____
_____
_____

"But the Lord is faithful, and he will
**strengthen you
and protect you**
from the evil one."

2 Thessalonians 3:3

Everlasting Life

God point out anything that offends You
and lead me along the path of everlasting life.

Are you ever concerned when you ask God to point things out in your life that offend Him?

_____
_____
_____
_____
_____
_____
_____
_____
_____

Can you be on the path of everlasting life if you are knowingly living a sinful life?

_____
_____
_____
_____
_____
_____
_____
_____
_____

*"See if there is any offensive way in me,
and lead me in the way **everlasting**."*

Psalm 139:24

FAITH TALK

Forgive, So You Will Be Forgiven

*I do not want any unforgiveness
to leave a dark spot on my soul.
I choose to forgive.*

Praying and turning the penalty of the offense over to God (Romans 12) is an act of your obedience to a command of God; it is an act of your love for God (John 14).

Were you aware of how important it is to forgive?

_____
_____
_____
_____
_____
_____
_____
_____
_____

Is there anyone you need to forgive or ask forgiveness from?

_____
_____
_____
_____
_____
_____
_____
_____
_____

"And when you stand praying, if you hold anything against anyone, **forgive them,** *so that your Father in heaven may forgive you your sins."*

Mark 11:25

Follow Me

Jesus does not tell me I
need to follow other Christians.

Have you ever fallen victim to this clever lie?

_____
_____
_____
_____
_____
_____
_____
_____
_____

How would you explain to an unbeliever that your obedience to Christ is not a form of bondage, but rather the beginning of true freedom?

_____
_____
_____
_____
_____
_____
_____
_____
_____

*"'Come, **follow me**,' Jesus said, 'and
I will send you out to fish for people.'"*

Matthew 4:19

FAITH TALK

Abound In Every Good Work

When I want to feel rich,

I will count all my blessings

money can't buy.

List all the blessings you have been given that money didn't buy:

_____
_____
_____
_____
_____
_____
_____
_____
_____
_____

Have these blessings also been poured into others? Explain:

_____
_____
_____
_____
_____
_____
_____
_____
_____

"And God is able to bless you abundantly, so that in all things at all times, having all that you need, you will **abound in every good work***"*

2 Corinthians 9:8

Wait Patiently

God does great things
through those surrendered to His will.

When do you remember surrendering to God's will?

_____
_____
_____
_____
_____
_____
_____
_____

Have you prayed for something in your own life only to see someone else you know receive it? Were you happy for them? Why or why not?

_____
_____
_____
_____
_____
_____
_____
_____
_____
_____

"Be still before the Lord
and **wait patiently** *for him;*
do not fret when people succeed in their ways,
when they carry out their wicked schemes."

Psalm 37:7

FAITH TALK

His Household

I am blessed because
of Whose I am; not
because of the things I have.

Explain how you are a member of God's Kingdom:

_____
_____
_____
_____
_____
_____
_____
_____
_____
_____

List the responsibilities involved in being a child of God:

_____
_____
_____
_____
_____
_____
_____
_____
_____
_____

"Consequently, you are no longer foreigners and strangers, but fellow citizens with God's people and also members of **his household***"*

Ephesians 2:19

Compassionate & Gracious God

Grace allows for my mistakes to serve a higher purpose, rather than a feeling of shame.

List a few benefits of the cross for you:
___
___
___
___
___
___
___
___

Jesus died on a cross in your place so you wouldn't have to feel shame. What higher purpose is grace playing in your life?
___
___
___
___
___
___
___
___
___
___

> 15 "But you, Lord, are a
> **compassionate and gracious God**,
> *slow to anger, abounding in love and faithfulness.*
> *16 Turn to me and have mercy on me;*
> *show your strength in behalf of your servant;*
> *save me, because I serve you*
> *just as my mother did."*
>
> Psalm 86:15-16

FAITH TALK

You Gave Me Life

Everything I have is because
of God's grace and favor.

Have you ever been tempted to earn God's favor? When?
_____
_____
_____
_____
_____
_____
_____
_____
_____

Why does God show you His grace and favor?
_____
_____
_____
_____
_____
_____
_____
_____

*"You gave me life and showed
me kindness, and in your
providence watched over my spirit."*

Job 10:12

Image: Bernardo Ramonfaur/Shutterstock.com

FAITH TALK

His Great Love For Us
I'm worth dying for!

Explain why Jesus went to the cross for you:

_____
_____
_____
_____
_____
_____
_____
_____

How would you explain God's plan for salvation to an unbeliever?

_____
_____
_____
_____
_____
_____
_____
_____

> "*But because of* **his great love for us**, *God, who is rich in mercy, 5 made us alive with Christ even when we were dead in transgressions—it is by grace you have been saved.*"
> Ephesian 2:4-5

Lamp of the Lord

The Holy Spirit is the lamp
of the Lord that sheds
light into my soul.

Write down the last time you heard the Lord whisper in your heart:

_____
_____
_____
_____
_____
_____
_____
_____
_____

Describe how you transmit this light into others' lives:

_____
_____
_____
_____
_____
_____
_____
_____
_____

"The human spirit is the
lamp of the Lord
that sheds light on one's inmost being."

Proverbs 20:27

FAITH TALK

Under Grace
I received grace,
so I will offer grace.

Explain a situation when you offered grace to someone. What were the circumstances?
_____
_____
_____
_____
_____
_____
_____
_____

Explain the last time you had to ask someone to extend grace to you. Was it difficult to ask for?
_____
_____
_____
_____
_____
_____
_____
_____
_____

*"For sin shall no longer be your master,
because you are not under*

the law, but **under grace**.*"*

Romans 6:14

Christian Life Coaching by LtA

Letter, Written On Our Hearts

My life is significant
and worth celebrating.

How has the Lord shown you that you are worth celebrating?

_____
_____
_____
_____
_____
_____
_____
_____
_____
_____

How do you celebrate the family and friendships God has provided you with?

_____
_____
_____
_____
_____
_____
_____
_____
_____
_____

"You yourselves are our
letter, written on our hearts,
known and read by everyone."

2 Corinthians 3:2

FAITH TALK

Many Rooms
Grace carries me all the way home!

Write down the emotions you feel when you know you are being received in the Kingdom of God:

_____
_____
_____
_____
_____
_____
_____
_____
_____

What did the party in heaven look like on the day of your repentance?

_____
_____
_____
_____
_____
_____
_____
_____
_____

> "Do not let your hearts be troubled.
> You believe in God; believe also in me.
> ² My Father's house has **many rooms**;
> if that were not so, would I have told you that
> I am going there to prepare a place for you?
> ³ And if I go and prepare a place for you,
> I will come back and take you to
> be with me that you also may be where I am.
> ⁴ You know the way to the place where I am going."

John 14:1-4

Righteousness of God

*My sin for His righteousness-
what a glorious exchange!*

Explain what you are receiving in this glorious exchange:

_____
_____
_____
_____
_____
_____
_____
_____
_____
_____

With Jesus taking on your sin debt and paying it in full, are you fully living out the righteous life He died to give you? Explain:

_____
_____
_____
_____
_____
_____
_____
_____
_____
_____

*"God made him who had no sin to be sin for us,
so that in him we might become the*
righteousness of God.*"*

2 Corinthians 5:21

FAITH TALK

His Face Shine On You
God loves me extravagantly!

Describe the ways that God shows His extravagant love:
_____
_____
_____
_____
_____
_____
_____
_____
_____
_____

Describe the ways you show your extravagant love for Him:
_____
_____
_____
_____
_____
_____
_____
_____
_____
_____

[24] *"The LORD bless you and keep you;* [25] *the LORD make* **his face shine on you** *and be gracious to you;* [26] *the LORD turn his face toward you and give you peace."*

Numbers 6:24-26

Come To Call The Sinners

Christians shouldn't be busy
only serving saved people
and blessing blessed people!

Where should Christians be serving?

_____

_____

_____

_____

_____

_____

_____

_____

_____

In 1 Peter 4, Peter addresses the importance of serving God. How should you be administering God's grace?

_____

_____

_____

_____

_____

_____

_____

"It is not the healthy who need a doctor, but the sick.
I have not **come to call the righteous***, but sinners."*

Mark 2:17

FAITH TALK

As The Lord Forgave You

I will forgive who and
what hurt me; I want
the *lesson* to *bless* me.

Describe a "blesson" you recently experienced:
_____
_____
_____
_____
_____
_____
_____
_____
_____

Explain how you would describe a "blesson" to an unbeliever:
_____
_____
_____
_____
_____
_____
_____
_____

*"Bear with each other and forgive
one another if any of you has a
grievance against someone. Forgive*
as the Lord forgave you."

Colossians 3:13

My Portion & My Cup

God has provided exactly what I need.

Describe a time when God showed up in a supernatural way to provide for you:

_____
_____
_____
_____
_____
_____
_____
_____

Has God used you to provide for someone else? Explain:

_____
_____
_____
_____
_____
_____
_____
_____

"Lord, you alone are
my portion and my cup;
you make my lot secure."

Psalm 16:5

FAITH TALK

Cleanse Our Consciences

Who I am from God's perspective:
redeemed, reconciled, renewed,
reborn, holy, righteous…

List some other adjectives that describe who you are from God's perspective:

_____
_____
_____
_____
_____
_____
_____
_____
_____

List some adjectives of Who God is from your perspective:

_____
_____
_____
_____
_____
_____
_____
_____
_____

"*How much more, then, will the blood of Christ,
who through the eternal Spirit offered himself unblemished to God,*

cleanse our consciences

*from acts that lead to death,
so that we may serve the living God!*"

Hebrews 9:14

For My Benefit

I will confess my sin to God,
repent and then let it go.
I will not punish myself for
something God has chosen to forget.

Below, write a confession, repent and then declare that this is in the past and as God chooses to forget, so will you:

_____
_____
_____
_____
_____
_____
_____
_____
_____
_____

Have you ever known someone who just won't let it go? How would you explain to them the importance of releasing the person and event into God's hands?

_____
_____
_____
_____
_____
_____
_____
_____
_____
_____

"*Surely it was* **for my benefit**
*that I suffered such anguish. In your love you
kept me from the pit of destruction;
you have put all my sins behind your back.*"

Isaiah 38:17

FAITH TALK

In the Gap

Part of succeeding as a believer involves
ample intercession for others in
your prayer life. I choose to stand in the gap.

You have a great privilege as a Christian to intercede in prayer for others. List the people for whom you feel led to intercede in prayer:

_____
_____
_____
_____
_____
_____
_____
_____
_____

Are you aware of anyone who stood in the gap for you? Explain:

_____
_____
_____
_____
_____
_____
_____
_____
_____
_____

"I looked for someone among them who would build up the wall and stand before me **in the gap** *on behalf of the land so I would not have to destroy it, but I found no one."*

Ezekiel 22:30

Future Generations

I want to be a blessing
to future generations.

Explain how you can actively be a blessing from this day forward for future generations in your family and friends:

_____
_____
_____
_____
_____
_____
_____
_____
_____

Were you ever aware that someone in your life was a blessing to you and you didn't even know it until years later? Explain:

_____
_____
_____
_____
_____
_____
_____
_____
_____

"Let this be written for a
future generation,
*that a people not yet
created may praise the Lord"*

Psalm 102:18

FAITH TALK

Quarrels Among You

I am blessed,
not entitled.

Explain how being a child of God entitles you to an inheritance Christ freely gives you but does not entitle you to live a sinful life:

_____
_____
_____
_____
_____
_____
_____
_____

How would you explain this to an unbeliever?

_____
_____
_____
_____
_____
_____
_____

*"What causes fights and **quarrels among you**? Don't they come from your desires that battle within you? 2 You desire but do not have, so you kill. You covet but you cannot get what you want, so you quarrel and fight. You do not have because you do not ask God. 3 When you ask, you do not receive, because you ask with wrong motives, that you may spend what you get on your pleasures."*

James 4:1-3

Desire Of The Afflicted

Jesus, You are the only
One who can fill
the hole in my soul.

Have you longed for something, and until Christ entered your life, you had a hole in your soul?

_____
_____
_____
_____
_____
_____
_____
_____
_____

How have you found Solomon's discovery in Ecclesiastes 2 to be true - that no earthly pleasure truly satisfies your soul? Explain:

_____
_____
_____
_____
_____
_____
_____
_____
_____

"You, Lord, hear the
desire of the afflicted;
you encourage them, and
you listen to their cry"

Psalm 10:17

FAITH TALK

Going Astray

When I stray from You,
gently remind me
You are the Great I Am!

To what extent are we responsible to keep watch over one another's souls?

_____
_____
_____
_____
_____
_____
_____
_____
_____
_____

Jesus is the Good Shepherd. Explain a time when you felt like you had strayed from God and how He received you when you returned to Him:

_____
_____
_____
_____
_____
_____
_____
_____
_____
_____
_____

*'For you were like sheep **going astray**,'*
but now you have returned to the
Shepherd and Overseer of your souls."

1 Peter 2:25

Wisdom From God

Free and dead no longer;
reborn and alive in Christ;
what a supernatural conversion!

Do you remember the day you received Christ?
_____
_____
_____
_____
_____
_____
_____
_____
_____
_____

Write down the details of that day:
_____
_____
_____
_____
_____
_____
_____
_____
_____
_____

*"It is because of him that you are in Christ Jesus,
who has become for us*
wisdom from God—*that is,
our righteousness, holiness and redemption."*

1 Corinthians 1:30

FAITH TALK

Healing

Wounds don't heal if I keep re-opening them.
I will give God time to completely heal me.

Describe how God healed a wound you incurred once you handed it over to Him:

_____
_____
_____
_____
_____
_____
_____
_____
_____
_____

Do you believe God has not lost His ability to heal, and His love for His people has not diminished? Why or why not?

_____
_____
_____
_____
_____
_____
_____
_____
_____
_____

> "Then your light will break forth like the dawn,
> and your **healing** will quickly appear;
> then your righteousness will go before you,
> and the glory of the Lord will be your rear guard."
>
> Isaiah 58:8

The Lord's Great Love

Don't ruin a good today by
thinking about a bad yesterday.
His grace and mercy
is new every morning!

Do you have to fight the habit of meditating on something that has already happened even though you know His grace and mercy is new every morning?

_____
_____
_____
_____
_____
_____
_____
_____

What habit could you form to help remind you of his grace and mercy each morning?

_____
_____
_____
_____
_____
_____
_____
_____

22 Because of **the Lord's great love** we are not consumed, for his compassions never fail.
23 They are new every morning;
great is your faithfulness.

Lamentations 3:22-23

FAITH TALK

Servant of Christ

It is OK to live a life
others don't understand.

Describe a moment in time when you realized it is your one and only life here on earth and you chose to live it for the Lord:

_____
_____
_____
_____
_____
_____
_____
_____
_____
_____
_____

How would you explain to an unbeliever your reasons for faith in Christ?

_____
_____
_____
_____
_____
_____
_____
_____
_____
_____

"Am I now trying to win the approval of human beings, or of God? Or am I trying to please people? If I were still trying to please people,
I would not be a **servant of Christ**.*"*

Galatians 1:10

Peace At All Times

I will forgive even if they aren't sorry;
because I deserve peace.

Is an apology important to you?

_____
_____
_____
_____
_____
_____
_____
_____

What would help you be more forgiving?

_____
_____
_____
_____
_____
_____
_____
_____
_____

"Now may the Lord of peace himself give you
peace at all times
and in every way.
The Lord be with all of you."

2 Thessalonians 3:16

FAITH TALK

Forgive

When I forgive, I don't change the past.
I change the future.

Explain how you are changing the future when you forgive:

_____
_____
_____
_____
_____
_____
_____
_____
_____
_____

Why do you think forgiveness is such an obstacle for so many people?

_____
_____
_____
_____
_____
_____
_____
_____
_____
_____

*[14] "For if you **forgive** other people when they sin against you, your heavenly Father will also forgive you. [15] But if you do not forgive others their sins, your Father will not forgive your sins."*

Matthew 6:14-15

Christian Life Coaching by LtA

Prayer Offered in Faith
TGIF
Thank God I'm forgiven!

Write down as many adjectives as you can that describe how being forgiven of your sins makes you feel:

_____
_____
_____
_____
_____
_____
_____
_____
_____

Now describe how Jesus might feel knowing He made you feel this way:

_____
_____
_____
_____
_____
_____
_____
_____
_____

"And the **prayer offered in faith**
will make the sick person well;
the Lord will raise them up. If they
have sinned, they will be forgiven."

James 5:15

FAITH TALK

More Than Conquerors
God deeply loves me!

If you knew you were going to die, what would you want to relay to others?

___

What connection does this have to your heart?

___

> 37 "No, in all these things we are ***more than conquerors*** through him who loved us. 38 For I am convinced that neither death nor life, neither angels nor demons, neither the present nor the future, nor any powers, 39 neither height nor depth, nor anything else in all creation, will be able to separate us from the love of God that is in Christ Jesus our Lord."
>
> Romans 8:37-39

Christian Life Coaching by LtA

Eternal Life

My self-worth is determined by
Jesus' finished work on the cross.

List the people you still allow to determine your self-worth and why:

___
___
___
___
___
___
___
___
___
___

List the ways God shows His love for you:

___
___
___
___
___
___
___
___
___
___

*"For God so loved the world that
he gave his one and only Son,
that whoever believes in him
shall not perish but have*
eternal life."

John 3:16

FAITH TALK

Finds Mercy

I will not shift blame, so I can receive life-changing forgiveness through my repentance and have continued fellowship with God.

If you were able to change one thing in your life, what would it be? Why?

___
___
___
___
___
___
___
___
___

How does it feel when you know you are out of fellowship with God?

___
___
___
___
___
___
___
___
___
___

"Whoever conceals their sins does not prosper, but the one who confesses and renounces them **finds mercy**.*"*

Proverbs 28:13

God's Throne of Grace

Shame says that I'm flawed
and undeserving, grace says
because I'm flawed I am cherished.

Explain how God uses the flawed to declare the Good News to the ends of the earth:

_____
_____
_____
_____
_____
_____
_____
_____
_____
_____

Do your imperfections strengthen your ability to declare the Good News or inhibit it? Explain:

_____
_____
_____
_____
_____
_____
_____
_____

"Let us then approach **God's throne of grace** *with confidence, so that we may receive mercy and find grace to help us in our time of need."*

Hebrews 4:16

FAITH TALK

Down From Heaven

God has an answer
to a fallen world.

Describe how you are part of God's answer to this fallen world:

___

How do you explain to people their battles will be Christ's victory?

___

'For I have come **down from heaven**
not to do my will but to do the
will of him who sent me."

John 6:38

Glorify Your Father

How am I pollinating my world?

Have you ever wondered how every gesture, tone of voice, every act of kindness is pollinating your world?

_____
_____
_____
_____
_____
_____
_____
_____

List some tangible ways to magnify God in your day-to-day life:

_____
_____
_____
_____
_____
_____
_____

"In the same way, let your light shine before others, that they may see your good deeds and

glorify your Father

in heaven."

Matthew 5:16

FAITH TALK

God Forgave You
I will make forgiveness a
daily offering in my life.

Describe a recent event that required you to forgive someone:
_____
_____
_____
_____
_____
_____
_____
_____
_____
_____

Have you ever doubted God's forgiveness once you confessed, prayed and repented? If so, why?
_____
_____
_____
_____
_____
_____
_____
_____
_____
_____

*"Be kind and compassionate to
one another, forgiving each other,
just as in Christ*
God forgave you."

Ephesians 4:32

Image: Amanda Carden/Shutterstock.com

FAITH TALK

Strongholds

Jesus doesn't help me
manage my strongholds.
He sets me free from them!

Describe a stronghold the enemy had on you from which Jesus set you free:

_____
_____
_____
_____
_____
_____
_____

How would you explain to an unsaved person the fact that sin forms a chain that only the Savior can break?

_____
_____
_____
_____
_____
_____
_____
_____

*"The weapons we fight with are not
the weapons of the world. On the
contrary, they have divine
power to demolish* **strongholds**.*"*

2 Corinthians 10:4

The Lord Upholds

Just because I had
a bad moment doesn't
make me a bad person.

Do you ever feel like you disappoint God? When? Why?

_____
_____
_____
_____
_____
_____
_____
_____
_____
_____

Explain why you are worthy of receiving grace because of a bad moment:

_____
_____
_____
_____
_____
_____
_____
_____
_____
_____

"though he may stumble,
he will not fall,
for the Lord upholds
him with his hand."

Psalm 37:24

FAITH TALK

The Word Became Flesh

When writing the story
of my life, only Jesus
can hold the pen.

Who do you allow to define you?

_____
_____
_____
_____
_____
_____
_____
_____
_____
_____

Who do you have in your life that helps keep you focused on Jesus?

_____
_____
_____
_____
_____
_____
_____
_____
_____
_____

"The Word became flesh
*and made his dwelling among us. We have
seen his glory, the glory of the one and only
Son, who came from the Father, full of
grace and truth."*

John 1:14

The Lord Weighs The Heart

God is more concerned
about my heart
than my performance.

Describe a time when you thought you had to perform for God:
___
___
___
___
___
___
___
___
___

Explain how David was a man after God's own heart:
___
___
___
___
___
___
___
___
___

"*A person may think their own ways are right, but* **the Lord weighs the heart.**"

Proverbs 21:2

FAITH TALK

Inherit a Blessing

I cannot control what people say
about me or how they treat me.
But I can control how I respond.

Is God's personal involvement in creation giving you hope for the world today?

_____
_____
_____
_____
_____
_____
_____
_____
_____
_____

Do you believe God is in charge of your reputation or are people?

_____
_____
_____
_____
_____
_____
_____
_____
_____

"Do not repay evil with evil or insult with insult.
On the contrary, repay evil with blessing,
because to this you were called so that you
may **inherit a blessing.**"

1 Peter 3:9

Thorns

I will remember Who wore the thorns
if I start complaining about my life.

Describe how you feel knowing what Jesus paid for your life:
_____
_____
_____
_____
_____
_____
_____
_____

Do you think Jesus went to the cross for you so you could feel shame and guilt? Guilt is a result of violation of God's laws according to the Bible. What is the ultimate solution to guilt?
_____
_____
_____
_____
_____
_____
_____

"*and then twisted together a crown of* **thorns**
*and set it on his head. They put a staff
in his right hand. Then they knelt in front
of him and mocked him.
'hail, king of the Jews!' they said.*"

Matthew 27:29

FAITH TALK

Your Hand Will Guide Me

Jesus pursues me,
redeems me,
brings me home!

Explain the day when the trumpet shall sound:

_____
_____
_____
_____
_____
_____
_____
_____

What emotions well up in you knowing Jesus is returning to bring you home?

_____
_____
_____
_____
_____
_____
_____
_____

[7] *"Where can I go from your Spirit? Where can I flee from your presence?*
[8] *If I go up to the heavens, you are there; if I make my bed in the depths, you are there.*
[9] *If I rise on the wings of the dawn, if I settle on the far side of the sea,*
[10] *even there* **your hand will guide me**,
your right hand will hold me fast."

Psalm 139:7-10

The Resurrection And The Life

I can rest in the finished
work of the cross.

If all you do is struggle through life then what was the cross for?

_____
_____
_____
_____
_____
_____
_____
_____
_____

How do you defend your peace during trials to an unbeliever?

_____
_____
_____
_____
_____
_____
_____
_____
_____

"Jesus said to her, **'I am the resurrection and the life**. *The one who believes in me will live, even though they die'"*

John 11:25

FAITH TALK

His Hand Is Stretched Out
God's grace goes far
beyond sin's disgrace.

Do you believe you are right now separated or united with Christ? Explain:
_____
_____
_____
_____
_____
_____
_____
_____

If you have anyone in your life that tries to disgrace you for any reason, write a prayer below releasing them from this shameful act and allow God's grace to flow over and in you:
_____
_____
_____
_____
_____
_____
_____
_____

For the Lord Almighty has purposed, and who can thwart him?
His hand is stretched out,
and who can turn it back?"

Isaiah 14:27

He Chose Us

God created me to be the focus of His love.

Do you have to wait to enjoy heaven? Explain:
_____
_____
_____
_____
_____
_____
_____
_____
_____
_____

Did your eternal life begin the day of salvation? Explain:
_____
_____
_____
_____
_____
_____
_____
_____
_____
_____

4 "**For he chose us** in him before the creation of the world to be holy and blameless in his sight. In love 5 he predestined us for adoption to sonship through Jesus Christ, in accordance with his pleasure and will"

Ephesians 1:4-5

FAITH TALK

A Man After My Own Heart

My heart sustains me,
my sin does not define me.

How was Saul not a man after God's own heart? How was David a man after God's own heart?

_____
_____
_____
_____
_____
_____
_____
_____
_____
_____
_____

Are you quick to repent? Why or why not?

_____
_____
_____
_____
_____
_____
_____
_____
_____

"After removing Saul, he made David their king. God testified concerning him: 'I have found David son of Jesse, **a man after my own heart;** *he will do everything I want him to do.'"*

Acts 13:22

Free From Sin

I cannot knowingly out sin
God's ability to forgive me.

Do you live like the fact that you are free? Explain:

_____
_____
_____
_____
_____
_____
_____
_____
_____
_____

How would you explain this freedom in Christ to an unbeliever?

_____
_____
_____
_____
_____
_____
_____
_____
_____

"because anyone who has died has been set **free from sin**.*"*

Romans 6:7

FAITH TALK

Confess My Transgressions

Thinking I can cover my sin breaks fellowship
with God. The wonderful interchange
is when I confess and repent from my sin.
God then covers it and remembers it no longer.

Did you ever think you could hide something from God? Explain the outcome:

_____
_____
_____
_____
_____
_____
_____
_____
_____

Why do you think God chooses not to remember our repented sin?

_____
_____
_____
_____
_____
_____
_____
_____
_____

*"Then I acknowledged my sin to you and did
not cover up my iniquity. I said, "I will*

confess my transgressions

to the Lord. "And you forgave the guilt of my sin."

Psalm 32:5

Christian Life Coaching by LtA

I Will Answer Him
The will of God won't lead me
where His grace won't keep me.

Describe a time that God asked you to do something you felt ill-equipped to attempt:

_____
_____
_____
_____
_____
_____
_____
_____
_____
_____
_____

What can we learn from the life of Noah? His obedience? God's grace? God's judgement?

_____
_____
_____
_____
_____
_____
_____
_____
_____

"He will call on me, and
I will answer him;
I will be with him in trouble,
I will deliver him and honor him."

Psalm 91:15

FAITH TALK

Make You Known

People remember how
I make them feel.

How do you show God is in you?

_____
_____
_____
_____
_____
_____
_____
_____

Is your interaction with people authentic? What happens to your witness if you are just going through the motions?

_____
_____
_____
_____
_____
_____
_____
_____

*"I have **made you known** to them,*
and will continue to make you known in
order that the love you have for me may
be in them and that I myself may be in them."

John 17:26

And The Dust Returns

God became man and died
for the dust He created.

Explain how Jesus' sacrifice has impacted your life?

_____
_____
_____
_____
_____
_____
_____
_____
_____
_____
_____

How would your life's meaning change if you didn't have the hope of a permanent home with Jesus?

_____
_____
_____
_____
_____
_____
_____
_____
_____
_____
_____

*"**and the dust returns**
to the ground it came from,
and the spirit returns to God who gave it."*

Ecclesiastes 12:7

FAITH TALK

Declare His Glory

Everywhere I go is
my mission field.

Do you believe that you were called for mission work? Why or why not?

_____
_____
_____
_____
_____
_____
_____
_____
_____
_____
_____

Do you have a mission to make disciples? To glorify Christ? To build up believers?

_____
_____
_____
_____
_____
_____
_____
_____
_____
_____
_____

*"**Declare his glory**
among the nations,
his marvelous deeds among all peoples."*

Psalm 96:3

You Knit Me Together

I will let go of hurtful words spoken
over me years ago that have
affected my worth and purpose.

If you are holding onto untrue hurtful words that are still penetrating your heart, write them down here. Then pray over the loss, pray over the person or people who have hurt you and forgive them:

___
___
___
___
___
___
___
___
___

If you have caused anyone pain that affected their worth and purpose, write another prayer asking for forgiveness for this behavior:

___
___
___
___
___
___
___
___
___

"For you created my inmost being;
you knit me together
in my mother's womb."

Psalm 139:13

FAITH TALK

Hope In Christ

Being born into a family that is angry, controlling,
oppressive and non-believers doesn't
mean God's grace isn't sufficient to end the cycle.

Are you a first generation believer? If so, you are drawing the bloodline of Jesus over your life. You have an extraordinary chance to affect future generations that will be watching you intently. Describe your feelings concerning this responsibility:

_____
_____
_____
_____
_____
_____
_____
_____
_____

Explain your understanding of the power of the Blood in your life:

_____
_____
_____
_____
_____
_____
_____
_____
_____

"in order that we, who were the first to put our
hope in Christ,
might be for the praise of his glory."

Ephesians 1:12

To The Only Wise God Be Glory

God's will is progressive
as I grow in Christlikeness.

What does it mean to you that you are growing in Christlikeness?

_____
_____
_____
_____
_____
_____
_____
_____
_____

What happens to your witness if you are not focused on growing in Christlikeness?

_____
_____
_____
_____
_____
_____
_____
_____
_____

26 "but now revealed and made known through the prophetic writings by the command of the eternal God, so that all the Gentiles might come to the obedience that comes from faith— 27 **to the only wise God be glory** *forever through Jesus Christ! Amen."*

Romans 16:26-27

FAITH TALK

Lavished
My status in heaven
is child of God.

The world loves titles and status. How does your status in heaven make you feel?

_____
_____
_____
_____
_____
_____
_____
_____
_____
_____

How would you explain being a child of God to an unbeliever?

_____
_____
_____
_____
_____
_____
_____
_____
_____
_____

"See what great love the Father has **lavished** *on us, that we should be called children of God! And that is what we are!"*

1 John 3:1

East Is From The West

My mistakes are no
surprise to God,
I need only to repent.

Are you still hard on yourself when you make a mistake?

_____
_____
_____
_____
_____
_____
_____
_____
_____

Can you see your mistakes as merely a means to make corrections, and not failures? Why or why not?

_____
_____
_____
_____
_____
_____
_____
_____
_____

"as far as the
east is from the west,
*so far has he removed our
transgressions from us."*

Psalm 103:12

FAITH TALK

Scripture Fulfilled

God requires me to believe,
He's done the rest.

Do you believe that Jesus' work on the cross is His finished work for us to believe in? Why?

_____
_____
_____
_____
_____
_____
_____
_____
_____
_____

Is picking up your cross and following Jesus some burden you must carry: a strained relationship, a thankless job, a physical illness, etc. or is it an absolute surrender, dying to self? Explain:

_____
_____
_____
_____
_____
_____
_____
_____

"*Later, knowing that everything had now been finished, and so that* **Scripture would be fulfilled**, *Jesus said, 'I am thirsty.'*"

John 19:28

Edification

May my words lift others up!

Make a list of the words that help heal and lift others up:

_____
_____
_____
_____
_____
_____
_____
_____
_____
_____

Make another list of the people who need to hear these words:

_____
_____
_____
_____
_____
_____
_____
_____
_____
_____

"Let us therefore make every effort to do what leads to peace and to mutual **edification**.*"*

Romans 14:19

FAITH TALK

Justified

I am not my shame,
I am a redeemed child of God!

Does your justified spiritual position before God impact your reality today? Explain:

_____
_____
_____
_____
_____
_____
_____
_____
_____

Describe situations where people are still trying to shame you. Are you standing firm in your faith?

_____
_____
_____
_____
_____
_____
_____
_____
_____

*"and all are **justified** freely
by his grace through the
redemption that came by Christ Jesus"*

Romans 3:24

Love Your Enemies

I will not stop appreciating my life
when someone treats me badly,
I will pray for them and move on.

Describe a time that you recently showed mercy to someone:

_____
_____
_____
_____
_____
_____
_____
_____
_____

Explain the difference between mercy and grace:

_____
_____
_____
_____
_____
_____
_____
_____

"But I tell you,
love your enemies
*and pray for those
who persecute you"*

Matthew 5:44

FAITH TALK

Justice

God dispenses perfect justice;
I will see my foes not as God's failures, but as His projects;
they are His concern-not mine.

Explain a time when you were able to just walk away, wish someone well and asked God to take over and prayed for them:

_____
_____
_____
_____
_____
_____
_____
_____
_____
_____

God's justice and mercy are seemingly incompatible. Justice involves the dispensing of deserved punishment, and mercy is pardoning with compassion for a sinner. How do these two attributes of God form a unity within His character?

_____
_____
_____
_____
_____
_____
_____
_____

"For I, the Lord, love **justice**; I hate robbery and
wrongdoing. In my faithfulness I will reward
my people and make an everlasting covenant with them."

Isaiah 61:8

Double Portion

Only God can repay what has been taken
from me. I will stop trying to collect from anyone else.

If you've been hurt, you often try to feel better by making someone else prove something to you so you won't get hurt again. Describe what you think that makes the other person feel like:

_____
_____
_____
_____
_____
_____
_____

Write a prayer asking God to forgive you for demanding payment from someone who doesn't owe you:

_____
_____
_____
_____
_____
_____
_____

"*Instead of your shame you will receive a double portion,
and instead of disgrace you will rejoice in your inheritance.*
And so you will inherit a **double portion** *in your land,
and everlasting joy will be yours.*"

Isaiah 61:7

FAITH TALK

Faithful & Just

What I've done doesn't change who God is.
Any guilt and condemnation is from the enemy.
God loves me unconditionally!

Is the enemy trying to convince you that you are still not good enough?

_____
_____
_____
_____
_____
_____
_____
_____
_____

List some major causes of guilt. Are you vigilantly slamming the door on these attacks? Why or why not?

_____
_____
_____
_____
_____
_____
_____
_____
_____
_____

"If we confess our sins, he is **faithful and just** *and will forgive us our sins and purify us from all unrighteousness."*

1 John 1:9

See The Kingdom Of God

Deliverance from self requires
being consumed with God,
less occupied with my sin, and
finding rest in the Jesus' work on the cross.

Is there anything you could be contributing to in order to provide a positive outcome of a present circumstance you are facing?

_____
_____
_____
_____
_____
_____
_____
_____
_____

How are you being consumed with God? Is it working?

_____
_____
_____
_____
_____
_____
_____
_____
_____

"Jesus replied, 'Very truly I tell you, no one can **see the kingdom of God** unless they are born again.'"

John 3:3

FAITH TALK

Let Them Pray

Prayer invokes the Holy Spirit to heal
our wounds and rid us of emotional
and spiritual contamination.

Are you using prayer as a last resort or a first line of defense? Explain:

___

When you worship the Lord, do you find you reconnect with Him emotionally and spiritually? Do you need to worship Him more?

___

"Is anyone among you in trouble?
Let them pray. Is anyone happy?
Let them sing songs of praise."

James 5:13

Healed

By His wounds I am healed!

Have you faced mistreatment because of your faith? Did anyone encourage you? What did they do?

_____
_____
_____
_____
_____
_____
_____
_____

How is Jesus helping you live a righteous life?

_____
_____
_____
_____
_____
_____
_____
_____

> "'He himself bore our sins' in his body on the cross, so that we might die to sins and live for righteousness; 'by his wounds you have been **healed**.'"

1 Peter 2:24

FAITH TALK

Immense Patience

Like Paul, may I never forget for a
moment that I am a sinner held in
God's arms and crowned with His love.

What motivates you more, the love of God and promise of life with Him eternally, or the threat of hell?

_____
_____
_____
_____
_____
_____
_____
_____
_____

Explain the embrace of the Lord:

_____
_____
_____
_____
_____
_____
_____
_____

15 *"Here is a trustworthy saying that deserves full acceptance: Christ Jesus came into the world to save sinners—of whom I am the worst. 16 But for that very reason I was shown mercy so that in me, the worst of sinners, Christ Jesus might display his* **immense patience** *as an example for those who would believe in him and receive eternal life."*

1 Timothy 1:15-16

Crucified With Christ

Who I've been is far less important
than who I'm becoming.

Describe some of the changes you have undergone since being born again:

_____
_____
_____
_____
_____
_____
_____
_____
_____
_____

Do these changes cause you anxiety or peace? Explain:

_____
_____
_____
_____
_____
_____
_____
_____

"I have been **crucified with Christ**
*and I no longer live, but Christ lives
in me. The life I now live in the
body, I live by faith in the Son of God,
who loved me and gave. himself for me."*
Galatians 2:20

FAITH TALK

Offering Your Gift

To receive God's blessings I cannot
have unrepentant sin in my heart.

Do you have, or do you know someone who has unrepentant sin?

How does this cause you to be out of fellowship with God?

"Therefore, if you are **offering your gift**
*at the altar and there remember
that your brother or sister
has something against you"*

Matthew 5:23

Perfect

If I'm looking for perfection
Christ is my example.

I won't burden myself or anyone else to carry the cross of perfection.
Have you ever expected other Christians to be perfect?

How did that make them feel? Were you disappointed?

"Be perfect, therefore, as your heavenly Father is **perfect***."*

Matthew 5:48

FAITH TALK

Yoke of Slavery

It's for freedom Christ set us free.
I will stand firm in this truth and
not let myself be burdened ever
again by the yoke of slavery.

What does the yoke of slavery mean to you?
_____
_____
_____
_____
_____
_____
_____
_____
_____
_____

What causes you to be yoked in this way?
_____
_____
_____
_____
_____
_____
_____
_____
_____
_____

*"It is for freedom that Christ has set us free.
Stand firm, then, and do not let
yourselves be burdened again by a*
yoke of slavery.*"*

Galatians 5:1

Forgetting What Is Behind

I won't worry about making
mistakes because God's
grace is sufficient.

I will enjoy the scenery on my detour as God works things out for my good.
How will God turn your detour into a great destination? Explain:
___
___
___
___
___
___
___
___

Do detours prove God's involvement in your life or do they cause you to worry and doubt? Explain:
___
___
___
___
___
___
___
___

"Brothers and sisters, I do not consider myself yet to
have taken hold of it. But one thing I do:
Forgetting what is behind
and straining toward what is ahead"

Philippians 3:13

FAITH TALK

Unfading Beauty

The beauty I desire is the kind
you see showing from the inside out.

How do people describe your countenance?

_____
_____
_____
_____
_____
_____
_____
_____
_____

When you see a person's unpleasant facial expressions, how does that make you view their heart, their life, their testimony?

_____
_____
_____
_____
_____
_____
_____
_____
_____

3 "Your beauty should not come from outward adornment, such as elaborate hairstyles and the wearing of gold jewelry or fine clothes. 4 Rather, it should be that of your inner self, the **unfading beauty** *of a gentle and quiet spirit, which is of great worth in God's sight."*

1 Peter 3:3-4

Advancing God's Work

The outcome of my challenges
magnify God's supply of
grace to make it through them.

Describe a challenge that seemed impossible to overcome and only by God's grace you were able to:
___
___
___
___
___
___
___
___

How would you explain God supplying the exact amount of grace you need each day to an unbeliever?
___
___
___
___
___
___
___
___

*"Or to devote themselves to myths and endless genealogies.
Such things promote controversial speculations rather than*
advancing God's work—*which is by faith."*

1 Timothy 1:4

FAITH TALK

Attitude Of Your Minds

Forgiveness changes
the present not the past.

Explain when you forgive someone how that changes you attitude and heart:

_____
_____
_____
_____
_____
_____
_____
_____
_____
_____

Explain how unforgiveness changes your attitude and heart:

_____
_____
_____
_____
_____
_____
_____
_____

"to be made new in the

attitude of your minds"

Ephesians 4:23

Apostleship
Being obedient to God's
will is not difficult.

Unbelievers tell Christians that it is too hard to follow Christ. They complain about the things they have to give up. How are you answering these statements?

_____
_____
_____
_____
_____
_____
_____
_____
_____
_____

Have you ever felt being obedient to Christ was a challenge? Explain:

_____
_____
_____
_____
_____
_____
_____
_____
_____
_____

*"Through him we received grace and **apostleship** to call all the Gentiles to the obedience that comes from faith for his name's sake."*

Romans 1:5

FAITH TALK

Not Everything Is Beneficial

Grace can be abused when a
Christian exercises their
liberty without using discernment.

Are you, or do you know a Christian that lives solely under grace and expects to remain in fellowship with God regardless of how they live? Explain:

___

Do believers face consequences from their sin behavior?

___

[23] "'I have the right to do anything,' you say—but
not everything is beneficial.
'I have the right to do anything'—but not everything is constructive. [24] No one should seek their own
good, but the good of others."

1 Corinthians 10:23-24

My Portion Forever

I can claim His promises
when I feel I have disappointed
myself or someone else.

It feels terrible to let someone down. How do you rebound when you see disappointment on someone's face? Explain:

_____
_____
_____
_____
_____
_____
_____
_____
_____

How do you encourage someone who has let you down?

_____
_____
_____
_____
_____
_____
_____
_____

*"My flesh and my heart may fail,
but God is the strength of my heart*
and **my portion forever**."

Psalm 73:26

FAITH TALK

Trials and Joy

Why is it important to remain joyful during trials? James 1:2-3 tells us to *"Consider it pure joy, my brothers and sisters, whenever you face trials of many kinds, ³ because you know that the testing of your faith produces perseverance."* Joy and pain can exist together. We do not have to deny our pain in our suffering to remain joyful in the Lord. Trials, though difficult, are short-lived in comparison to eternity. If we focus on God's deliverance rather than on our trials, we can be a light to a dark fallen world.

As we walk with Christ on our journey, there is so much to rejoice over; namely, our eternal inheritance, our transformation, increasing our intimacy with God, growing in obedience, eternity spent with Christ our Lord, genuineness of our faith, the refinement trials brings us, deepening our dependence on God, dying to self, progress toward Christlikeness, reward of faithfulness, fellowship with other believers, building the kingdom, broadening our faith, our future glory, to name a few. Keep your first love, the love of Christ, as your focus and you will be able to withstand the sway of this world and be a valuable witness to the saving grace found only in the Lord Jesus Christ.

Praying this section of apparent paradox enlightens you of how your loving relationship with Jesus Christ will carry you through your trials. Believers in Christ can remain joyful during trials!

Image: Amanda Carden/Shutterstock.com

FAITH TALK

Divine Nature

Joy keeps me usable; sorrow keeps me merciful;
trials make me resilient; failures
keep me reliant; God keeps me going!

Can you encourage and counsel others now who are going through trails and perhaps have doubt about God's love because of going through their trial?

_____
_____
_____
_____
_____
_____
_____
_____
_____

Are you living with the divine nature God created you with? Explain:

_____
_____
_____
_____
_____
_____
_____
_____

"For since the creation of the world God's invisible qualities—his eternal power and **divine nature**—*have been clearly seen, being understood from what has been made, so that people are without excuse."*

Romans 1:20

Crown of Life

On difficult days, when I feel inadequate,
unloved and unworthy, I will raise my
head and remember Whose daughter I am.

Describe what being the daughter of the King means to you:

_____
_____
_____
_____
_____
_____
_____
_____
_____

Do you feel eternally secure in your salvation and receiving the crown of life as God promised? Why or why not?

_____
_____
_____
_____
_____
_____
_____
_____

> *"Blessed is the one who perseveres under trial because, having stood the test, that* person will receive the **crown of life** that *the Lord has promised to those who love him."*

James 1:12

FAITH TALK

Ever Present Help

It is very comforting
to know God
has my back.

Describe a time when someone betrayed you and you called out to God and He answered:

_____
_____
_____
_____
_____
_____
_____
_____
_____

What does the word refuge make you think of? Have you ever tried to find security in things other than God?

_____
_____
_____
_____
_____
_____
_____
_____
_____

"God is our refuge and strength,
*an **ever-present***
***help** in trouble."*

Psalm 46:1

Christian Life Coaching by LtA

There Was No Guest Room

We're all innkeepers-
this heart has prepared Him room.

Life is busy and unpredictable, is Jesus still the center of your life?

_____
_____
_____
_____
_____
_____
_____
_____

Satan loves to keep us running in circles. If he can distract us, he can minimize our usefulness to the Kingdom of God. What distractions are you currently under?

_____
_____
_____
_____
_____
_____
_____
_____

"and she gave birth to her firstborn, a son. She wrapped him in cloths and placed him in a manger, because

there was no guest room

available for them."

Luke 2:7

FAITH TALK

Wait Quietly

God's delay is for His display.
His timing is always perfect.

Sometimes we think what appears to be a "no" is actually a waiting period when God is saying "not yet?" Have you been in a waiting period?

_____
_____
_____
_____
_____
_____
_____
_____
_____
_____

Have you asked God to operate on your schedule? Have you been disappointed when He doesn't?

_____
_____
_____
_____
_____
_____
_____
_____

25 *"The Lord is good to those whose hope
is in him, to the one who seeks him;*

26 *it is good to* **wait quietly**
for the salvation of the Lord."

Lamentations 3:25-26

Christian Life Coaching by LtA

Keeping His Promise
God keeps His promises!

Have you ever doubted that God keeps His promises? If so, why?

___
___
___
___
___
___
___
___

A person who has truly repented from rejection of Christ to faith in Christ will give evidence of a changed life. What fruit have you produced as evidence that you have a changed life?

___
___
___
___
___
___
___
___

"The Lord is not slow in
keeping his promise,
as some understand slowness.
Instead he is patient with you,
not wanting anyone to perish,
but everyone to come to repentance."

2 Peter 3:9

FAITH TALK

The Oppressed

The Lord will guide me as
I heal from my past
and I will enjoy every
moment in His presence.

What is the upside of your present wound? Is it forcing you into closer fellowship with the Lord? Explain:

___
___
___
___
___
___
___
___
___
___

Describe righteousness and justice as some of God's attributes:

___
___
___
___
___
___
___
___
___
___

"The Lord works righteousness
and justice for all
the oppressed."

Psalm 103:6

He Who Began A Good Work...

*I am a work in progress
and God is not
done with me yet!*

Does remaining unfinished exhilarate or upset you? Explain:

_____
_____
_____
_____
_____
_____
_____

Who do you know that has patiently waited on God to move in their lives? How has their example impacted you?

_____
_____
_____
_____
_____
_____
_____

"being confident of this, that
he who began a good work
*in you will carry it on to completion
until the day of Christ Jesus."*

Philippians 1:6

FAITH TALK

Horn Of My Salvation

My emotions are not
reliable but scripture is.
Do you run for the throne when you are emotional or do you turn to an unreliable source? Explain:

_____
_____
_____
_____
_____
_____
_____
_____
_____
_____

In 2 Peter 1 we are told the Bible in infallible; it is absolutely trustworthy. How would you explain to an unbeliever the Bible is the infallible Word of God, inerrant, authoritative, reliable and sufficient to meet our needs?

_____
_____
_____
_____
_____
_____
_____
_____

*"The Lord is my rock, my fortress and my deliverer;
my God is my rock, in whom I take refuge, my shield and the*
horn of my salvation, *my stronghold."*

Psalm 18:2

Complacent

Just because I found
God doesn't mean I
should stop seeking Him.

Complacency breeds captivity.
Do you only seek God when you are in a trial? Do you seek God's hand or His face? Explain:

What do you do to hear from God? What have you heard lately?

"At that time I will search Jerusalem with
lamps and punish those who are **complacent**,
who are like wine left on its dregs, who think,
'The Lord will do nothing, either good or bad.'"

Zephaniah 1:2

FAITH TALK

Pierced For Our Transgressions

God holds up my soul,
He binds my heartache,
He makes me whole.

Do you ask people to restore you to wholeness? What is the outcome when you leave God out of the equation? Explain:

_____
_____
_____
_____
_____
_____
_____
_____
_____
_____

Do you believe this verse is referring to spiritual or physical healing, or both?

_____
_____
_____
_____
_____
_____
_____
_____
_____
_____

"But he was **pierced for our transgressions**,
he was crushed for our iniquities;
the punishment that brought us peace was on him, and by
his wounds we are healed."

Isaiah 53:5

He Remains Faithful

I remember praying for
the things I have now.

List things you prayed for that God provided for you:

_____
_____
_____
_____
_____
_____
_____
_____
_____

Who is praying for you right now? Who are you praying for right now?

_____
_____
_____
_____
_____
_____
_____
_____
_____

"if we are faithless,
he remains faithful,
for he cannot disown himself."

2 Timothy 2:13

FAITH TALK

It Will Be Yours

Worrying will not change
the outcome; but prayer will.

Describe the difference from how you felt when you worried and meditated with a problem rather than praying and releasing the outcome to God:

_____
_____
_____
_____
_____
_____
_____
_____
_____
_____

God does not want us to carry around the weight of problems and burdens. In the space provided, list any problems and burdens you are presently carrying and vow to release them to God:

_____
_____
_____
_____
_____
_____
_____
_____

"Therefore I tell you, whatever you ask for in prayer, believe that you have received it, and

it will be yours."

Mark 11:24

The Marks Of Jesus

My scars indicate I'm
Stronger than what
tried to hurt me.

Are your scars a reminder or a testimony of what tried to hurt you? Explain:

_____
_____
_____
_____
_____
_____
_____
_____

What signs of commitment to Jesus do you possess?

_____
_____
_____
_____
_____
_____
_____
_____

*"From now on, let no one cause
me trouble, for I bear on my body*
the marks of Jesus.*"*

Galatians 6:17

FAITH TALK

Hope & A Future

God's plans for my
life far exceed
today's circumstances.

Do you believe your circumstances are meant to harm you or prepare you? Explain:

_____
_____
_____
_____
_____
_____
_____
_____
_____

Has your suffering given you opportunities to share your faith that you wouldn't otherwise have had?

_____
_____
_____
_____
_____
_____
_____
_____
_____

"For I know the plans I have for you,"
declares the Lord, "plans to prosper you
and not to harm you, plans to
give you **hope and a future**.*"*

Jeremiah 29:11

Think About Such Things

> I will not injure my
> eyesight by looking
> at the bright side.

Is it difficult to trust God during trials? If yes, why? If no, how have you grown in your ability to trust God during trials?

_____
_____
_____
_____
_____
_____
_____
_____
_____
_____

What can you appreciate right now?

_____
_____
_____
_____
_____
_____
_____
_____
_____
_____

"Finally, brothers and sisters, whatever is true, whatever is noble, whatever is right, whatever is pure, whatever is lovely, whatever is admirable—if anything is excellent or praiseworthy— **think about such things**.*"*
Philippians 4:8

FAITH TALK

Crown of Beauty

My healing is a process
God walks with me
through if I let Him.

How is God shaping you? Can you cooperate with Him more in the process?

_____
_____
_____
_____
_____
_____
_____
_____
_____

Let God have your ashes you don't need them anymore! Explain what ashes you are releasing:

_____
_____
_____
_____
_____
_____
_____
_____
_____
_____
_____

"and provide for those who grieve in Zion—
to bestow on them a **crown of beauty**
instead of ashes, the oil of joy instead of mourning,
and a garment of praise instead of a spirit of despair.
They will be called oaks of righteousness"

Isaiah 61:3

Fire

God does not always prevent
me from the fire but He
will preserve me through it!

Are you walking through a fire right now? Do you believe God will preserve you through it? Explain:

_____
_____
_____
_____
_____
_____
_____
_____
_____

Deuteronomy 4 describes God as a consuming fire. This fire consumes and destroys anything unholy. Why do you think it's important to be held to the flame?

_____
_____
_____
_____
_____
_____
_____
_____
_____

"They saw that the **fire** had not harmed their bodies,
nor was a hair of their heads singed;
their robes were not scorched,
and there was no smell of fire on them."

Daniel 3:27

FAITH TALK

Bore Our Suffering

God bears my burdens!

Describe a time when you were aware of God bearing your burdens for you:

___

Has anyone ever told you that your present suffering is because of your sin and disobedience? How did you respond to this?

___

"Surely he took up our pain
and **bore our suffering***,*
yet we considered him punished by God,
stricken by him, and afflicted."

Isaiah 53:4

Image: Freedom Studio /Shutterstock.com

FAITH TALK

Hushed

When I'm only looking at
the pain, I miss the Promise.

If God allows this storm to rage on I trust Him to calm me through it.
Do you know of any storm without end? Do you trust God to deliver you through life's storms?

_____
_____
_____
_____
_____
_____
_____

Pain is one of God's ways of reaching us. Was His voice above a whisper during the pain? If so, why do you think so?

_____
_____
_____
_____
_____
_____
_____
_____

"He stilled the storm to a whisper;
the waves of the sea were **hushed**.*"*

Psalm 107:29

Stand On The Earth

My redeemer lives!
You worship an omnipotent, omnipresent living God!
Describe how you feel knowing Jesus lives in you:

_____
_____
_____
_____
_____
_____
_____
_____
_____
_____

If Satan hates our progress toward Christlikeness, explain how you will continue to fight the good fight of faith:

_____
_____
_____
_____
_____
_____
_____
_____
_____
_____

*"I know that my redeemer lives,
and that in the end he will*
stand on the earth."

Job 19:25

FAITH TALK

A Time To...

People of faith may be torn apart
but we get sewn back together!

Describe a time when you felt torn apart and God stitched you back together:

_____
_____
_____
_____
_____
_____
_____
_____

What question would Jesus ask you about your faith? What level of intimacy are you pursuing with Him?

_____
_____
_____
_____
_____
_____
_____
_____

"a time to tear and a time to mend,
a time to be silent and ***a time to*** *speak"*

Ecclesiastes 3:7

Wounds

Something happens between
a wound and a scar;
it's called a healing.

A scar from what hurt us can be turned into a mark of Who healed us. Do you trust God to bind up your wounds? If so, has the wound been rewritten into a signature of Christ?

_____
_____
_____
_____
_____
_____
_____
_____
_____

Do you have expectations about how God works? Is He obligated to perform according to these expectations?

_____
_____
_____
_____
_____
_____
_____
_____

*"He heals the brokenhearted
and binds up their **wounds**."*

Psalm 147:3

FAITH TALK

Shield & Rampart

I have immunity and am
sheltered from evil.

Explain a time that you felt God sheltering you from evil:

_____
_____
_____
_____
_____
_____
_____
_____
_____
_____

Do you believe in demons and their work today? How do you respond when you're attacked spiritually?

_____
_____
_____
_____
_____
_____
_____
_____
_____

*"He will cover you with his feathers,
and under his wings you will find refuge;
his faithfulness will be your*
shield and rampart."

Psalm 91:4

Called

God brings unexpected good out of
undesirable situations.

Do you believe that you deserve better than your present circumstance? Do you trust God to bring you through this trial?

_____
_____
_____
_____
_____
_____
_____
_____
_____

Is there an area of your life you need healing - emotional, spiritual, physical, financial? Do you believe Jesus is dispensing compassion and mercy in response to your plea?

_____
_____
_____
_____
_____
_____
_____
_____
_____

> "And we know that in all things God works for the good of those who love him, who have been ***called*** according to his purpose."

Romans 8:28

FAITH TALK

Every Tear

Salvation turns my
mourning into rejoicing.

Describe your best day before Christ and then describe your worst day with Christ:

_____
_____
_____
_____
_____
_____
_____
_____
_____
_____

Has the reality of heaven and your escape from eternal imprisonment really set in?

_____
_____
_____
_____
_____
_____
_____
_____
_____
_____

*"He will wipe **every tear** from their eyes.
There will be no more death' or mourning or
crying or pain, for the old order
of things has passed away."*

Revelation 21:4

Everlasting Arms

I'm stronger where
I've been broken.

God allows life storms to strengthen me and bring me to a place of reliance in Him.

Is your life invested in shakeable or unshakeable things? Explain:

_____
_____
_____
_____
_____
_____
_____
_____

Why would God leave some mountains unmovable?

_____
_____
_____
_____
_____
_____
_____
_____
_____

*"The eternal God is your refuge,
and underneath are the* **everlasting arms***.
He will drive out your enemies before you,
saying, 'Destroy them!'"*

Deuteronomy 33:27

FAITH TALK

Given Me Hope

When I'm rejected by others;
I know You understand how that feels.

How did Jesus react to being rejected?

_____
_____
_____
_____
_____
_____
_____

Has anyone distanced themselves from you because of your love of Christ? If so, did this cause you to embrace Him more or less? Do you think God used this situation to draw you closer to Him?

_____
_____
_____
_____
_____
_____
_____
_____

> 49 *"Remember your word to your servant,*
> *for you have* **given me hope**.
> 50 *My comfort in my suffering is this:*
> *Your promise preserves my life.*
> 51 *The arrogant mock me unmercifully,*
> *but I do not turn from your law.*
> 52 *I remember, Lord, your ancient laws,*
> *and I find comfort in them."*

Psalm 119:49-52

Restoration

People will criticize, God will consecrate;
People will shame, God will save;
People will hurt, God will honor.

Have you ever put faith into anything or anyone other than God? What was the result?

_____
_____
_____
_____
_____
_____
_____
_____
_____

The Parable of the Prodigal Son found in Luke 15 is a picture of a father receiving a son back into a relationship. Is there any relationship to which the Father is asking you to bring restoration?

_____
_____
_____
_____
_____
_____
_____
_____
_____

"*But I will* **restore** *you to health and heal your wounds,' declares the Lord*"

Jeremiah 30:17

FAITH TALK

Righteous Right Hand

God allows me to go the edge
of destruction so I will know
the joy of His deliverance!

Describe the last time God rescued you:

_____
_____
_____
_____
_____
_____
_____
_____
_____
_____

Have you fully grasped the magnitude of God's love for you? What impact has this love had on you?

_____
_____
_____
_____
_____
_____
_____
_____
_____

*"So do not fear, for I am with you; do not
be dismayed, for I am your God.
I will strengthen you and help you;
I will uphold you with my*
righteous right hand."

Isaiah 41:10

Get Up!

I demonstrate my faith by worshipping God
before any battles and
confidently enter the challenge
I face inspired to victory!

Do you pray and worship before starting each day? Do your days differ when you do and when you don't? Explain:

_____
_____
_____
_____
_____
_____
_____
_____
_____

What is the evidence you trust God?

_____
_____
_____
_____
_____
_____
_____
_____
_____

14 "*His friend responded, 'This can be nothing other than the sword of Gideon son of Joash, the Israelite. God has given the Midianites and the whole camp into his hands.'*
15 *When Gideon heard the dream and its interpretation, he bowed down and worshiped. He returned to the camp of Israel and called out, '***Get up***! The Lord has given the Midianite camp into your hands.'"*

Judges 7:14-15

FAITH TALK

Deep Waters

God you are always guiding and
comforting me through
my darkest of days.

When you are in deep waters, is it friends and family or is it God you cry out to? How do the responses differ?

_____
_____
_____
_____
_____
_____
_____
_____
_____
_____

How do you comfort yourself in your distress? Do you have any regrets over your choice of comfort?

_____
_____
_____
_____
_____
_____
_____
_____
_____
_____

"In my distress I called to the Lord; I cried to my God for help. From his temple he heard my voice; my cry came before him, into his ears He reached down from on high and took hold of me;

*he drew me out of **deep waters**."*

Psalm 18:6, 16

He Cares For You

Worrying won't stop the bad stuff from happening-
but it will stop me from enjoying the good stuff.

Life is meant to be enjoyed and shared. Building up walls might keep the bad stuff out but it will also keep the good stuff from coming in.
Have you built up any walls you need to tear down? Explain:

_____
_____
_____
_____
_____
_____
_____
_____

Are there any obstacles in your life preventing you from having deep fellowship with God? Have you asked God to remove these obstacle?

_____
_____
_____
_____
_____
_____
_____
_____
_____

"Cast all your anxiety on him because
he cares for you."

1 Peter 5:7

FAITH TALK

Refined By Fire

Trials on my trails
deepen my experience with God.

Do you see trials as something meant for disrupting God's plan for your life, or for learning obedience? Explain:

___
___
___
___
___
___
___
___

In Genesis 12, Abram was called into unfamiliar territory. Has God called you to go anywhere uncomfortable and unfamiliar? If so, are you going?

___
___
___
___
___
___
___
___

6 "In all this you greatly rejoice, though now for a little while you may have had to suffer grief in all kinds of trials. 7 These have come so that the proven genuineness of your faith—of greater worth than gold, which perishes even though **refined by fire**—*may result in praise, glory and honor when Jesus Christ is revealed."*

1 Peter 1:6-7

He Will Not Return To Me

Grief can become destructive.

David reminds us to not allow our grief to continue without resolution. *Describe a time your grief was so powerful that you thought you would not overcome it:*

_____
_____
_____
_____
_____
_____
_____
_____
_____

Constructive sorrow, or Godly sorrow, can lead to change. Explain how God guided you through that difficult time:

_____
_____
_____
_____
_____
_____
_____
_____
_____

"But now that he is dead, why should I go on fasting? Can I bring him back again? I will go to him, but **he will not return to me**."

2 Samuel 12:23

FAITH TALK

I Will Praise You!

I worship the Lord
with all my heart.

Describe ways you praise and worship the Lord:

___
___
___
___
___
___
___
___
___
___

How does the authority of scripture get expressed in your life?

___
___
___
___
___
___
___
___
___
___

"I will praise you, Lord
*my God, with all my heart;
I will glorify your name forever."*

Psalm 86:12

The Lord Will Provide

Panic is the enemy's tool
to make me doubt God's provision.

Describe a time that the enemy tried to get you to panic over God's provision:

_____
_____
_____
_____
_____
_____
_____
_____

Was the enemy able to gain a foothold? If not, what tactics did you use to not lose any ground to him?

_____
_____
_____
_____
_____
_____
_____
_____

"So Abraham called that place
The Lord Will Provide. And to this day it is said,
'On the mountain of the Lord it will be provided.'"

Genesis 22:14

FAITH TALK

The Lord Hears

When life strikes a blow and
I stumble to my knees,
I'm now in the perfect
position to pray and praise.

Describe a time that you were on your knees crying out to the Lord and He heard you:

_____
_____
_____
_____
_____
_____
_____
_____

What does holding fast to the Word look like in your day to day?

_____
_____
_____
_____
_____
_____
_____
_____

"The righteous cry out, and
the Lord hears *them;*
he delivers them from all their troubles."

Psalm 34:17

The Lord Sustains Me

God's ultimate hug:
I love you no matter what;
you are precious to me.

I can stay as long as I want in His embrace!
Explain when you realized that God is the one that sustains you:

_____
_____
_____
_____
_____
_____
_____
_____
_____

How did you come to know your need for God?

_____
_____
_____
_____
_____
_____
_____
_____

4 *"I call out to the Lord,*
and he answers me from his holy mountain.
5 I lie down and sleep;
I wake again, because
the Lord sustains me."

Psalm 3:4-5

FAITH TALK

Brokenhearted

Only God can heal
my brokenness.

Describe a time when you were broken and wanted a friend or family member to make it better. What was the result?

_____
_____
_____
_____
_____
_____
_____
_____
_____

Reaching our breaking point causes us to seek the Lord more sincerely. Is there any rebellion that remains in your heart? Are you willing to fully submit to the authority of Jesus?

_____
_____
_____
_____
_____
_____
_____
_____
_____

"The Lord is close to the **Brokenhearted** *and saves those who are crushed in spirit."*

Psalm 34:18

If You Believe

Prayer is the first line defense
not a last resort. I will
draw strength from heaven.

Are you using the privilege of prayer Jesus died to give you?
___
___
___
___
___
___
___
___
___

On a scale of 1-10, how would you rate your prayer life? How could you improve your prayer life?
___
___
___
___
___
___
___
___
___

"***If you believe****, you will receive whatever you ask for in prayer."*

Matthew 21:22

FAITH TALK

Lamp Burning
God is the light in my darkness.

Have you found yourself the only light in a room of darkness? Maybe in your circle of friends, family or workplace? Why would God have put you there?

_____
_____
_____
_____
_____
_____
_____
_____
_____

If people don't respond to your light, is that a statement of your ability to witness? Why or why not?

_____
_____
_____
_____
_____
_____
_____
_____
_____

"*You, Lord, keep my* **lamp burning**;
my God turns my darkness into light."

Psalm 18:28

Wait For The Lord

When I wait, You strengthen my heart.

Do you wait well? Do you think God is trying to refine something in you by delaying the outcome?

_____
_____
_____
_____
_____
_____
_____
_____
_____
_____

Waiting on the Lord is found throughout the Bible. We are told to wait with expectant hope.
Could the waiting period be to extend the goodness of the outcome?

_____
_____
_____
_____
_____
_____
_____
_____
_____

*"Wait for the Lord;
be strong and take heart*
and **wait for the Lord**."

Psalm 27:14

FAITH TALK

Righteousness, Peace & Joy

I will not depend on people for my
happiness because my joy is in the Lord!

Happiness is carnal, fleshly. Joy is holy and Spirit filled.
Have you ever placed your happiness in someone or something? What was the result?

_____
_____
_____
_____
_____
_____
_____
_____

Our joy cannot be taken away. As believers we are promised the constant presence of the Holy Spirit. If your joy is lacking, how can you actively pursue a closer more intimate relationship with God?

_____
_____
_____
_____
_____
_____
_____
_____

"For the kingdom of God is not a matter of eating and drinking, but of **righteousness, peace and joy** *in the Holy Spirit"*

Romans 14:17

Christian Life Coaching by LtA

Pure Joy
Painful experiences help me grow.

There is joy on the other side of pain.
Pain is a very thorough teacher. Describe a situation where your pain brought a breakthrough:

_____
_____
_____
_____
_____
_____
_____
_____
_____
_____

Do you know someone who is constantly negative? A whiner? A complainer? How would you gently explain God needs to be their lifeline?

_____
_____
_____
_____
_____
_____
_____
_____
_____
_____

*2 "Consider it **pure joy**, my brothers and sisters, whenever you face trials of many kinds, 3 because you know that the testing of your faith produces perseverance."*

James 1:2-3

FAITH TALK

In The Beginning…
I am grateful for God's
Word affecting my life.

When we lack gratitude it can be a breeding ground for murmuring and grumbling.
List the things for which you are grateful:

_____
_____
_____
_____
_____
_____
_____
_____
_____
_____

What are the benefits of a grateful heart?

_____
_____
_____
_____
_____
_____
_____
_____

"In the beginning
was the Word, and the Word was
with God, and the Word was God."

John 1:1

Image: Amanda Carden/Shutterstock.com

FAITH TALK

Closer Than A Brother

My true friends help
multiply my joy
and divide my sorrows.

Make a list of all the people in your life you consider true friends:

_____
_____
_____
_____
_____
_____
_____
_____
_____
_____

What are the common attributes in your list of true friends?

_____
_____
_____
_____
_____
_____
_____
_____
_____
_____

"One who has unreliable friends soon comes to ruin, but there is a friend who sticks ***closer than a brother.****"*

Proverbs 18:24

Glory In Our Sufferings

Suffering produces perseverance,
perseverance produces character,
character produces hope.

Explain how we glory in our sufferings:
_____
_____
_____
_____
_____
_____
_____
_____
_____
_____

Define perseverance, character and hope:
_____
_____
_____
_____
_____
_____
_____
_____
_____
_____

3 *"Not only so, but we also* **glory in our sufferings**, *because we know that suffering produces perseverance; 4 perseverance, character; and character, hope."*

Romans 5:3-4

FAITH TALK

Friends

I am filled with joy because
I know that I'm on speaking
terms with God.

Describe how you feel knowing you are a friend of Jesus:

_____
_____
_____
_____
_____
_____
_____
_____
_____
_____
_____

How would you explain the benefits of friendship with Jesus to an unbeliever?

_____
_____
_____
_____
_____
_____
_____
_____
_____
_____

*"I no longer call you servants, because a servant does not know his master's business. Instead, I have called you **friends**, for everything that I learned from my Father I have made known to you."*

John 15:15

Grudges

I will not hold onto a grudge
because it is allowing someone
to live rent free in my soul.

Is holding a grudge related to your faith?

_____
_____
_____
_____
_____
_____
_____
_____

If you are holding onto a grudge please write down what it is and vow to release this person and event from occupying space in your mind and heart:

_____
_____
_____
_____
_____
_____
_____
_____

"Do not seek revenge or bear a **grudge**
*against anyone among your people,
but love your neighbor as yourself.
I am the Lord."*

Leviticus 19:18

FAITH TALK

Do Not Grieve
Joy transcends my circumstances!

Describe a time when you realized what you were going through was momentary and your joy returned:

_____
_____
_____
_____
_____
_____
_____
_____
_____
_____

Is lack of joy sinful?

_____
_____
_____
_____
_____
_____
_____
_____

"Nehemiah said, 'Go and enjoy choice food and sweet drinks, and send some to those who have nothing prepared. This day is holy to our Lord. **Do not grieve***, for the joy of the Lord is your strength.'"*
Nehemiah 8:10

Help The Weak

I am happy when God
answers my prayers.

I am happier when God makes me an answer to prayer!
Describe a time when you realized you were an answer to someone's prayer:

_____
_____
_____
_____
_____
_____
_____
_____
_____

When you offered this help and hope to someone, did your personal journey with Christ help you to reach them?

_____
_____
_____
_____
_____
_____
_____
_____
_____

"In everything I did, I showed you that by this kind of hard work we must **help the weak***, remembering the words the Lord Jesus himself said: 'It is more blessed to give than to receive.'"*

Acts 20:35

FAITH TALK

Wages Of Sin

I am thankful for what I've
already received as well
as what I've escaped!

How do you feel knowing that you escaped an eternity of separation from God?

_____
_____
_____
_____
_____
_____
_____
_____
_____
_____

How would you explain to an unbeliever their present separation from God?

_____
_____
_____
_____
_____
_____
_____
_____
_____
_____

"For the **wages of sin**
*is death, but the gift of God is eternal
life in Christ Jesus our Lord."*

Romans 6:23

Blots Out

I will allow God
time to restore me.

I am a living testimony of His redeeming and restoring work!
Are you actively telling the lost your testimony of the redeeming love of the Lord?
_____
_____
_____
_____
_____
_____
_____
_____
_____
_____

Would the message of the cross change if God chose to remember our sins?
_____
_____
_____
_____
_____
_____
_____
_____
_____
_____

"I, even I, am he who **blots out**
*your transgressions, for my own sake,
and remembers your sins no more."*

Isaiah 43:25

FAITH TALK

Holy Life
I was created to fill a
purpose only I can fill!

How is the Lord revealing or revealed His calling for you?

_____
_____
_____
_____
_____
_____
_____
_____

What does it mean to you to live a holy life? Is it possible?

_____
_____
_____
_____
_____
_____
_____
_____

*"He has saved us and called us to a **holy life**—
not because of anything we have done but
because of his own purpose and grace.
This grace was given us in Christ Jesus
before the beginning of time,"*

2 Timothy 1:9

Repaid

It is a joy to bless someone who can't repay me.

I have sadly seen people in the grocery line who cannot afford their purchase and have to put things back. I keep gift cards, perfume samples, books, etc. to give to them on the spot.

How are you blessing those around you?

_____
_____
_____
_____
_____
_____

What is your motivation to love those who don't love you? Who or what has helped you to love the way God loves?

_____
_____
_____
_____
_____
_____

> 12 "Then Jesus said to his host, 'When you give a luncheon or dinner, do not invite your friends, your brothers or sisters, your relatives, or your rich neighbors; if you do, they may invite you back and so you will be repaid.
> 13 But when you give a banquet, invite the poor, the crippled, the lame, the blind,
> 14 and you will be blessed. Although they cannot repay you, you will be **repaid** at the resurrection of the righteous.'"

Luke 14:12-14

FAITH TALK

Content

If God hasn't created the next
opportunity for me I will continue to
worship Him where I'm at.

Are you frustrated the next door hasn't opened? Are you certain God hasn't kept you where you are for a reason?

_____
_____
_____
_____
_____
_____
_____
_____
_____

What are some attributes of contentment?

_____
_____
_____
_____
_____
_____
_____
_____
_____

11 "I am not saying this because I am in need, for I have learned to be **content** *whatever the circumstances. 12 I know what it is to be in need, and I know what it is to have plenty. I have learned the secret of being content in any and every situation, whether well fed or hungry, whether living in plenty or in want."*

Philippians 4:11-12

Who Shall Separate Us

*Trials and suffering clarify and
cleanse me; make me wiser and
give me opportunities to minister.*

Trials strengthen my faith and deepen my dependence on God. God doesn't allow trials to weaken us; they are to strengthen us and build our reliance on Him.

Describe a trial that deepened your dependence on God:

_____
_____
_____
_____
_____
_____
_____
_____
_____

Does God's discipline prove His involvement in our lives? Does this kind of love draw us closer to Him?

_____
_____
_____
_____
_____
_____
_____
_____
_____

> "**Who shall separate us** *from the love of Christ? Shall trouble or hardship or persecution or famine or nakedness or danger or sword?"*
>
> Romans 8:35

FAITH TALK

Reflection

Reflection allows me to see any growth
I've had. I will not feel condemned
by what I see, I will rejoice in
being alive in Christ!

List the changes you see in your reflection over the past 5 years:

_____
_____
_____
_____
_____
_____
_____
_____
_____
_____
_____

Do you feel convicted or condemned by what you see? Why?

_____
_____
_____
_____
_____
_____
_____
_____
_____
_____

"For now we see only a **reflection** *as in
a mirror; then we shall see face to face.
Now I know in part; then I shall know
fully, even as I am fully known."*

1 Corinthians 13:12

All The Truth

I desire to grow. Every
problem has a purpose
when I allow God to teach.

What does your spiritual growth plan include?

_____
_____
_____
_____
_____
_____
_____
_____
_____

Why is it important to have a spiritual growth plan?

_____
_____
_____
_____
_____
_____
_____
_____
_____

But when he, the Spirit of truth, comes, he will guide you into **all the truth**. *He will not speak on his own; he will speak only what he hears, and he will tell you what is yet to come."*

John 16:13

FAITH TALK

Love & Justice

Vengeance fixes my attention on life's worst moments. I will release my faith for justice through prayer.

Explain a time that you sought revenge for a wrong done to you:

___

Did you take action or did you release the situation and the person to the Lord?

___

"But you must return to your God;
maintain **love and justice**, *and*
wait for your God always."

Hosea 12:6

Christian Life Coaching by LtA

Satisfy The Faint

For the moments when I feel I have
no more strength I will let go
and let God rejuvenate me.

Describe the last time you let God refresh you:

_____
_____
_____
_____
_____
_____
_____

How did you feel before the refreshment from God? How did you feel after?

_____
_____
_____
_____
_____
_____
_____

"I will refresh the weary and **satisfy the faint**."

Jeremiah 31:25

FAITH TALK

Troubles

I will not despise the
hardship, I will
rejoice in His deliverance!

Are you worn out by the hardship or are you anticipating His deliverance?

_____
_____
_____
_____
_____
_____
_____
_____
_____
_____

How much time do you think about spending eternity with Jesus? What comes to mind?

_____
_____
_____
_____
_____
_____
_____
_____
_____
_____

*"The righteous person may have many **troubles**,
but the Lord delivers him from them all"*

Psalm 34:19

The Lord Is With You

I am someone's miracle,
someone's answer to prayer. God uses ordinary people for extraordinary things!

Why does God choose unlikely people? Have you ever felt inadequate to live out His call on your life?

_____
_____
_____
_____
_____
_____
_____
_____

Recall a time when you knew that God had used you in an extraordinary way:

_____
_____
_____
_____
_____
_____
_____

*"When the angel of the Lord appeared
to Gideon, he said,*
'The Lord is with you,
mighty warrior.'"

Judges 6:12

FAITH TALK

Openhanded

Opportunities to help Someone
surround me each day.

Are you keeping an eye out for opportunities to be used to meet a need?

_____
_____
_____
_____
_____
_____
_____
_____
_____

Have you prayed for someone to meet one of your needs? Did God deliver?

_____
_____
_____
_____
_____
_____
_____
_____

*"There will always be poor people in the land.
Therefore I command you to be* **openhanded**
*toward your fellow Israelites who are
poor and needy in your land."*

Deuteronomy 15:11

Christian Life Coaching by LtA

New Self

I am thankful for the Lord's
boundless grace and for continuing
to form me into His likeness.

List the likeness to Christ you hope to have become in the next 5 years:

___

Since coming to faith in Christ, what likeness to Christ has been developed in you?

___

*"and have put on the **new self**,
which is being renewed in knowledge
in the image of its Creator."*

Colossians 3:10

Approved

I am thankful for the revelation that
true joy comes from You
not from people or possessions.

Describe when you realized your joy was in the Lord not people or possessions:

_____
_____
_____
_____
_____
_____
_____
_____
_____

Do you remember what provoked this revelation?

_____
_____
_____
_____
_____
_____
_____
_____
_____

*"Go, eat your food with gladness, and drink your wine with a joyful heart, for God has already **approved** what you do."*

Ecclesiastes 9:7

Well-Watered

The only One that can satisfy my heart
is the One Who made it.

Describe the last time you felt truly satisfied:

_____
_____
_____
_____
_____
_____
_____
_____
_____

What was the circumstance or reason for the feeling?

_____
_____
_____
_____
_____
_____
_____

*"The Lord will guide you always;
he will satisfy your needs in a sun-scorched land
and will strengthen your frame.
You will be like a **well-watered** garden,
like a spring whose waters never fail."*

Isaiah 58:11

FAITH TALK

You Anoint
I am lavished in His blessings.

How is God's blessing different from that of friends or family members?
___
___
___
___
___
___
___
___
___
___

Describe the feeling of your cup overflowing:
___
___
___
___
___
___
___
___
___
___

> *"You prepare a table before me in the presence of my enemies.*
> **You anoint** *my head with oil; my cup overflows."*

Psalm 23:5

Never Die

My present situation
is not my final destination.

When you think about spending all eternity in the presence of the Lord, explain how that will look and feel:

_____
_____
_____
_____
_____
_____
_____
_____
_____
_____

How important are the lost to you?

_____
_____
_____
_____
_____
_____
_____
_____
_____
_____

*"and whoever lives by believing in
me will **never die**."*

John 11:26

FAITH TALK

I Wake Again

*My faith in God only grows
stronger when applied
over my life circumstances.*

I can own a bar of soap but if I don't apply the soap when bathing, it does not benefit me.

When you face a trial, do you pour over scripture to find the answer? If so, explain how scripture helped you apply the Truth over the situation:

_____
_____
_____
_____
_____
_____
_____
_____
_____
_____
_____

Do you believe God is able? Explain:

_____
_____
_____
_____
_____
_____
_____
_____

5 "I lie down and sleep; **I wake again**,
because the Lord sustains me.
6 I will not fear though tens of
thousands assail me on every side."

Psalm 3:5-6

Christian Life Coaching by LtA

Rest Secured

When I can't choose
my circumstances,
I will choose joy.

Explain the comfort you feel knowing that the Lord will not let you see decay:

_____
_____
_____
_____
_____
_____
_____
_____
_____
_____

Explain the peace that surpasses all understanding:

_____
_____
_____
_____
_____
_____
_____
_____
_____
_____

9 "Therefore my heart is glad and my tongue rejoices;
my body also will **rest secure**,
10 because you will not abandon me to the realm
of the dead, nor will you let your
faithful one see decay."

Psalm 16:9-10

FAITH TALK

Repay

I'm stronger in
my brokenness.

I've been poured out so God can fill me with Him. Kintsugi is the form of restoration that suggests an object, once rendered useless, could be reworked into a brilliant piece of art, made more valuable by its inherent flaws.

Are you ashamed of your brokenness or are you thrilled God sees your flaws as his masterpiece? Explain:

_____
_____
_____
_____
_____
_____
_____
_____
_____

What are the attributes of human flaws?

_____
_____
_____
_____
_____
_____
_____

*"I will **repay** you for the years the locusts have eaten—the great locust and the young locust, the other locusts and the locust swarm—my great army that I sent among you."*

Joel 2:25

Christian Life Coaching by LtA

Valleys
Valleys are where
battles are fought
and where I grow.

Do you despise the valleys or are you growing from each battle you enter?
_____
_____
_____
_____
_____
_____
_____
_____
_____

Do you believe God goes before you and fights for you?
_____
_____
_____
_____
_____
_____
_____
_____
_____

*"And David became famous after he returned
from striking down eighteen thousand
Edomites in the **Valley** of Salt."*

2 Samuel 8:13

FAITH TALK

The Time Is Near
The Holy Spirit is
the revealer of Truth.

Revelation comes through Him, not by my own works. The breakthroughs will come.

Do the prophecies fulfilled in Jesus increase your faith? Explain:

_____
_____
_____
_____
_____
_____
_____
_____
_____
_____

Are you merely hearing the blessings or are you accepting them in your heart?

_____
_____
_____
_____
_____
_____
_____
_____
_____
_____

"Blessed is the one who reads aloud the words of this prophecy, and blessed are those who hear it and take to heart what is written in it, because **the time is near**.*"*

Revelation 1:3

Weaknesses

I will rejoice in my weakness,
it keeps me reliant on God.

Are you ashamed of your weaknesses? Do you allow people to point them out to you?
_____
_____
_____
_____
_____
_____
_____
_____
_____
_____

Vow you will rejoice in your weaknesses:
_____
_____
_____
_____
_____
_____
_____
_____
_____

"That is why, for Christ's sake, I delight in **weaknesses**, in insults, in hardships, in persecutions, in difficulties. For when I am weak, then I am strong."

2 Corinthians 12:10

FAITH TALK

The Earth Give Way

The storms are to
strengthen me,
not defeat me.

Have you ever thrown in the towel? Explain:
_____
_____
_____
_____
_____
_____
_____
_____
_____
_____

What circumstance made you question God's absence during the trial?
_____
_____
_____
_____
_____
_____
_____
_____

"Therefore we will not fear, though
the earth give way
*and the mountains fall into
the heart of the sea"*

Psalm 46:2

Interests Of Others

My joy will increase when I stop
thinking about myself and
think of what I can do for others.

If you are trying to learn from someone else's growth, it probably isn't working. Are you creating your harvest by sowing into others?

___
___
___
___
___
___
___
___
___

How do you develop the mind of Christ?

___
___
___
___
___
___
___
___
___

4 *"not looking to your own interests
but each of you to the*

interests of the others.

*5 In your relationships with one
another, have the same mindset as Christ Jesus"*

Philippians 2:4-5

FAITH TALK

Stand Firm

God is big enough to
solve my problems.

Have you ever wondered if God is not showing up for some reason? Explain:

___

Is it possible that this is the best for this particular moment? Is the anticipation of the blessing to come worth the wait?

___

"'You will not have to fight this battle. Take up your positions; **stand firm** and see the deliverance the Lord will give you, Judah and Jerusalem. Do not be afraid; do not be discouraged. Go out to face them tomorrow, and the Lord will be with you.'"

2 Chronicles 20:17

Eternal Glory

I am not aware of any
storms without end,
this one will pass too.

Some tests take much longer to pass.
Are you travelling around a familiar mountain again? Could it be that you are not relying on the Lord's will, but rather on your own?

_____
_____
_____
_____
_____
_____
_____
_____

Do you believe God cares about you? Do you trust His ways? Explain:

_____
_____
_____
_____
_____
_____
_____
_____

"And the God of all grace, who called you to his **eternal glory** in Christ, after you have suffered a little while, will himself restore you and make you strong, firm and steadfast."

1 Peter 5:10

FAITH TALK

Strong & Courageous

I will not retreat in order to
avoid a challenge
God has placed in my life.

He leads, I follow, and our relationship will grow deeper.
Describe the last time you felt like retreating rather than pushing through:

_____
_____
_____
_____
_____
_____
_____
_____
_____
_____

What does being courageous look like? Describe a person in your life that demonstrates courageous behavior:

_____
_____
_____
_____
_____
_____
_____
_____
_____

"Have I not commanded you? Be
strong and courageous.
Do not be afraid; do not be discouraged, for
the Lord your God will be with you wherever you go."

Joshua 1:9

Raised With Christ

Contentment isn't the fulfillment
of what I want - it's the realization
of how much I already have.

Describe the last time you set your mind on earthly things rather than on things above:
___
___
___
___
___
___
___
___
___

How did your spirit feel during this time?
___
___
___
___
___
___
___
___
___

"Since, then, you have been **raised with Christ**,
*set your hearts on things above, where Christ is,
seated at the right hand of God.
2 Set your minds on things above, not on earthly things."*

Colossians 3:1-2

FAITH TALK

One Body
No one else is like me.

No one else can function in the body of Christ like me.
I am thankful to God for His wisdom to place me where He needs me.
When did you know that you made a divine connection? Explain:

___

What is the biggest difference Jesus has made in your life that you would share with an unbeliever?

___

*"Just as a body, though one, has many parts,
but all its many parts form **one body**,
so it is with Christ."*

1 Corinthians 12:12

Mighty Acts

A believable testimony of God's
grace, mercy and love
requires going through trials.

I won't run from a challenge, I will let it mature me.
Is there any sin that will keep you from running your race?

___
___
___
___
___
___
___
___

Write your testimony you can share to an unbeliever:

___
___
___
___
___
___
___
___

15 *"My mouth will tell of your righteous deeds,*
of your saving acts all day long—
though I know not how to relate them all.
16 I will come and proclaim your
mighty acts, *Sovereign Lord;*
I will proclaim your righteous deeds, yours alone."

Psalm 71:15-16

FAITH TALK

Twice As Much

Don't waste your pain; when
you turn the broken pieces
over to God He creates beauty.

Describe the mosaic of your life God is creating:

_____
_____
_____
_____
_____
_____
_____
_____
_____
_____

Do you need to say goodbye to any regret, doubt, shame, etc.? If so, write it down:

_____
_____
_____
_____
_____
_____
_____
_____
_____
_____

*"After Job had prayed for his friends,
the Lord restored his fortunes and gave him*
twice as much *as he had before."*

Job 42:10

Power Is Made Perfect

Thankful that the Lord's strength
and power will be
glorified in my weakness.

How does God's power in your weakness look? Describe:

_____
_____
_____
_____
_____
_____
_____
_____

Define God's power:

_____
_____
_____
_____
_____
_____
_____
_____

"But he said to me, 'My grace is sufficient for you, for my **power is made perfect** *in weakness.' Therefore I will boast all the more gladly about my weaknesses, so that Christ's power may rest on me."*

2 Corinthians 12:9

FAITH TALK

To Him Be the Glory

If God is asking me to do something
I feel completely inadequate to do
I will rejoice knowing He is working
through me to show His strength.

Describe a time you knew the Lord was flowing through you:

___

How are you serving the Lord?

___

"If anyone speaks, they should do so as one who speaks the very words of God. If anyone serves, they should do so with the strength God provides, so that in all things God may be praised through Jesus Christ. **To him be the glory** *and the power for ever and ever. Amen."*

1 Peter 4:11

Warnings

Whenever I feel like complaining,
I will remember the weight that
carries in the spiritual world.

Do you ever feel you've overlooked God's generosity? How generous has He been to you?

_____
_____
_____
_____
_____
_____
_____
_____
_____
_____

Write a prayer that tells the Lord how grateful you are for continuing to show grace and mercy to you:

_____
_____
_____
_____
_____
_____
_____
_____
_____

9 *"We should not test Christ, as some of them did—
and were killed by snakes. 10 And do not grumble,
as some of them did—and were killed by the destroying angel.
11 These things happened to them as examples and
were written down as* **warnings** *for us,
on whom the culmination of the ages has come."*

1 Corinthians 10:9-11

FAITH TALK

Life & Peace

When I stop focusing on the problem
and lift my eyes to focus on God, that
is when I transcend from carnality to holy living.

Is it easy to meditate on the problem instead of on God?

_____
_____
_____
_____
_____
_____
_____
_____
_____
_____

Vow that you will run to Him and stop focusing on what your flesh is telling you to do:

_____
_____
_____
_____
_____
_____
_____
_____
_____
_____

*"The mind governed by the flesh is death,
but the mind governed by
the Spirit is* **life and peace**.*"*

Romans 8:6

Equip You

God has matched me to the world
I'm in and given me
what I need to succeed.

Describe what your success looks like. Are the passions, talents and plans God placed in your heart part of the success?

_____
_____
_____
_____
_____
_____
_____
_____
_____
_____

Describe what succeeding as a Christian means to you:

_____
_____
_____
_____
_____
_____
_____
_____
_____

*"**equip you** with everything good for doing his will, and may he work in us what is pleasing to him, through Jesus Christ, to whom be glory for ever and ever. Amen."*

Hebrews 13:21

FAITH TALK

Straight Paths

Mistakes are the first
steps to learning the
correct path to take.

How do you respond to your mistakes? Do you try to cover them up? Do you blame others?

_____
_____
_____
_____
_____
_____
_____
_____
_____
_____

Explain the Christian way to deal with making a mistake:

_____
_____
_____
_____
_____
_____
_____
_____
_____
_____

*"in all your ways submit to him,
and he will make your **paths straight**."*

Proverbs 3:6

Good To All

Life is not always good,
but God is!

Do you believe God is good to all He has created? Explain:

_____
_____
_____
_____
_____
_____
_____
_____
_____
_____

Have you ever felt like God has withheld His goodness from you? Explain:

_____
_____
_____
_____
_____
_____
_____
_____
_____

"The Lord is **good to all***;
he has compassion on all he has made."*

Psalm 145:9

FAITH TALK

He Protects
Rejoice in the deliverance
of the hardship!
Does Jesus' second coming influence your actions or interactions with others?

_____
_____
_____
_____
_____
_____
_____
_____
_____
_____
_____

Describe what your homecoming will be like:

_____
_____
_____
_____
_____
_____
_____
_____
_____
_____

"**he protects** all his bones,
not one of them will be broken."

Psalm 34:20

Christian Life Coaching by LtA

Heirs

Suffering doesn't separate me
from Christ-it unites me with Him.

Has your suffering caused you to draw closer to God?
_____
_____
_____
_____
_____
_____
_____
_____
_____
_____

Describe how your suffering united you with Christ:
_____
_____
_____
_____
_____
_____
_____
_____
_____

*"Now if we are children, then we are **heirs**—
heirs of God and co-heirs with Christ,
if indeed we share in his sufferings in order
that we may also share in his glory."*

Romans 8:17

FAITH TALK

Salvation

When life gets rough,
I recognize God's faithfulness.

Are you recognizing His faithfulness to deliver you, or do you think God expects you to stay in a state of suffering?

_____
_____
_____
_____
_____
_____
_____
_____
_____
_____
_____

Have you forgotten how this all ends?

_____
_____
_____
_____
_____
_____
_____
_____
_____
_____

"For God did not appoint us to suffer wrath but to receive **salvation** *through our Lord Jesus Christ."*

1 Thessalonians 5:9

Conclusion

I pray this devotional/interactive journal has encouraged you in your journey toward deeper intimacy with God. I pray you feel more connected to Jesus, His Word, and with the Bible - the only infallible, inerrant Word of God. My prayer is that the *Faith Talk: Journaling with God; A Journey of Christian Faith* series will help you grow to love God and God's Word more than you already did.

John 14:26 *"But the Advocate, the Holy Spirit, whom the Father will send in my name, will teach you all things and will remind you of everything I have said to you."*

It has been a privilege to serve the Kingdom's purpose for this book. I pray God continue to bless you and yours.

May His grace and peace be with you always,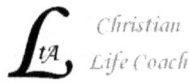

About the Author

LtA is a certified Christian Life Coach and Bible-study author. LtA teaches with a particular focus on purposeful living involving how to love and live based on God's Word. LtA shares biblical truths with practical applications people can apply to their lives. God has provided LtA opportunities to minister to people and share the gospel in pragmatic ways through *Christian Life Coaching by LtA* and the *Faith Talk* series. For more information on the author and this book please visit:

https://ChristianLifeCoachingbyLtA.com

Facebook

Twitter

Instagram

Pinterest

LinkedIn

About Kharis Publishing

Kharis Publishing is an independent, traditional publishing house with a core mission to publish impactful books, and channel proceeds into establishing mini-libraries or resource centers for orphanages in developing countries, so these kids will learn to read, dream, and grow. Every time you purchase a book from Kharis Publishing or partner as an author, you are helping give these kids an amazing opportunity to read, dream, and grow. Kharis Publishing is an imprint of Kharis Media LLC. Learn more at: https://www.kharispublishing.com.

www.ingramcontent.com/pod-product-compliance
Lightning Source LLC
Chambersburg PA
CBHW050513170426
43201CB00013B/1939